CERTAIN AS THE DAWN

Peter G. van Breemen, S.J.

DIMENSION BOOKS
Denville, New Jersey

1. meditation
2. Prayer

Imprimi potest: Johannes M. van Leeuwen, S.J.
Provincial of the Dutch Province
The Hague, July 31, 1980

Dedicated to the new Jesuit Community
Om Vuur
Deventer, The Netherlands

L.C. Catalog Card Number 80-68088

ISBN: 087193-131-1

TABLE OF CONTENTS

FOREWORD

Almost seven years after *As Bread that is Broken* and five years after *Called by Name* I feel the need to share another series of meditations on the Word of Life. Like the other two books this one has grown during a number of years, in various continents, through many people. It draws heavily from Scripture and from shared experience. I realize more and more how dependent we are on each other in all things, but especially in our faith. So much love, faith, insight, experience and challenge of numerous men and women have gone into this book, that I can hardly claim it as my own. Gratefully, in turn, I offer these chapters to those from whom I have received them and to all who seek and spread the Good News.

Like the other two books this one is centered around the free, creative love of God for us-as-we-are. We can be certain of this love, as we are certain of the dawn. God's goodness is at the origin of our days: once at the very beginning of them all, each day faithfully creating a new start, ready to lead us into the day that knows no sunset. I sincerely hope that every page may bring across the love of God and the joy of our faith.

Among the many who contributed on various levels and stages, three persons in the final phase stand out. First of all my sincere gratitude goes out to Sr. St. Thomas Wegmann, O.S.F. who with indefatigable and generous dedication assisted in manifold ways during the entire period of the actual writing. Next I want to express my appreciation to Sr. Bridget Haase, O.S.U. for her enthusiastic challenge, supportive criticism and stylistic corrections. Finally I thank Fr. Julian C. Resch, O. Praem. who was an excellent host and a reliable help.

ONE

GOD IS ALWAYS GREATER

The search for God today seems disguised. Often sought in numerous ways, his name is seldom spoken. Many thousands of people have 'turned East' in the hope of experiencing the *satori,* a certain immediacy with the Deepest Ground of being that brings the great enlightenment. There is a widespread interest in various forms of meditation; critics even speak of an 'interiority complex'. Solidarity with the poor and with those deprived of justice has become more manifest and outspoken. The promotion of peace arouses a tremendous interest. The liberation movement with its various focuses has become assertive. These look like new religions in secular forms.

Looking back we note that our ancestors invested much acumen, zeal and devotion in the proofs for God's existence. Yet these have little appeal to our generation. It is not so much the existence of God that is at stake for us, as it is the meaningfulness of those three letters. Used so often, the word has become hackneyed for many people. It is like a coin with its face worn-off. The word has been stretched so far that it has lost its substance. The word has been used in such inappropriate ways that it has become tainted and people have become allergic to it. Above all the keen awareness of much suffering, both in our immediate environment and on a world-wide scale, has often rendered the reality of God highly questionable. Is he real? Is he a psychological projection? Is he just the invention of the troubled heart?

Though we have been told that we are God's creation, we still cope with the suspicion that possibly God is no more than our creation. This idea after the first shock was welcomed as an enlightenment and a liberation. We had finally come to full stature! Gradually, however it seemed as though something essential had slipped away and that life had lost some of its thrust and vigor. Several psychiatrists have recently expressed their concern for a new form of neurosis caused by a lack of spirituality. Harvey Cox describes the evolution:

> I believe the current wave of skepticism about the human prospect and about our capacity to influence history is mainly the result of the modern assumption that human beings are fully responsible for everything that happens, that there is no higher intelligence or grander purpose at work in cosmic evolution and human history. The Turn East is the logical outcome of the death of God. This represents a curious twist in intellectual history. It was once argued by secular humanists that positing the existence of a deity makes human beings lazy, that they will merely sit back and let God do it. The other side of that coin, however, is that when the tasks become enormous and the challenges nearly overwhelming, it is not the presence of a cosmic ally but the lack of one that drives people to despair.[1]

A little parody expresses the same idea in a more satiric way. A traveler lost his way in the desert. Parched by the sun, he sees an oasis in the distance. "Ah," he thinks, "a mirage that is trying to delude me." He approaches the oasis but it fails to disappear. Clearly he sees the date palms, the grass, and even a spring. "Nothing but a thirst-illusion conjured up by my mind which has gone crazy! Such are the fantasies of one in my predicament. Projection! I even hear the sound of bubbling water. An audio-hallucination, no doubt. Oh, how cruel nature is!" A short time later two Bedouins find him dead. Said the one to the other, "The dates are almost dropping into his mouth, and yet he starved; the water from the spring runs at his side, yet he perished from thirst. How is this possible?" Answered the other, "He was a modern man who died from fear of projection."

Though exaggerated the tale has a point. The fear that God might be nothing but an indulgence of romanticism or an escape from life's hardships exists. Sometimes we also meet the conviction that belief in God is a cheap tranquilizer in frustrating moments or a bit of putty to fill up a gap where the mind falls short. The point often overlooked is that this fear of projection can have depressing and stifling effects.

On the other hand, this does not mean that the fear of projection is altogether out of place, as illustrated by the following experience of a graduate student. In one of the first sessions of a directed retreat he told the director that he envisioned God as a huge ice cube with a little light in the center. The retreat director could not make much sense of it and let it go for the time being. Towards the end of the retreat the young man himself referred to it saying that he had discovered *he* was the ice cube with the light in the center. He then explained that he was quite popular among his fellow students. Yet he had the feeling that it was impossible for them to touch base with him. He felt like an attractive light shielded by an enormous crust of ice. The retreat became fruitful when he discerned this projection, purified his image of God and clarified his understanding of self.

While every instance of projection is not as marked as this student's, we must acknowledge some projection in our every image of God. We see him 'as in a mirror'. Our human condition prevents us from seeing God as he is. This does not mean that any one image is as good as another nor that we should not try to reduce the amount of projection. It does mean that we shall never completely escape projection until we see him face to face.

The same human condition that causes us to create our own divine images - however inadequate - also destroys them from time to time. In some perceptive and sensitive diary notes written after his wife died of cancer, C. S. Lewis[2] compares our idea of God with a house of cards. If we are careful and adroit

enough we can build elaborate structures. But because our images of the Holy easily become idols, they have to be knocked
down now and then. God therefore occasionally shakes the
table on which our house of cards is placed, and the 'temple'
falls apart. Thus the Lord shows himself to be 'the great icono
clast'. "Could we not almost say that this shattering is one of the
marks of his presence?" For Lewis, the death of his wife was a
traumatic experience in which his image of God crumbled. It
took him some time to realize that this too was a grace.

The experience in which we feel like having lost God himself, because our image of him collapsed, is painful. Yet it will
not prevent us from starting another house of cards. We simply
cannot do without it for any length of time. The new image will
integrate the effects of the last shattering experience. It will express how we assimilated the suffering. Sometimes the new picture of God will portray him as cruel or tyrannical. It requires a
genuine faith to recognize the positive element in pain, to keep
trusting even in distress, and to rebuild a constructive image of
God after another disappointment. The new image however will
eventually share the lot of the previous ones. It breaks down.
After having recovered again, we will begin once more - such
are we.

If it is true that to a certain extent we make our images of
God, it is no less true and probably more important, that our
images of God make us. Eventually we become like the God we
image. A person who thinks of God as a despotic superpower
imposing all kinds of hardships on his people will become fear-
ful, slavish and possibly quite exacting of his fellowmen. If
one's idea of God is very impersonal, religion will be non-committal and vague as well. The God of predestination evokes a
gloomy but hard-working people. Providence conceived of as a
divine operation which does not allow for any human interven-
tion creates a fundamentalist way of life with its puritanical
laws. The belief in God as Abba nurtures confident, free persons. The God of love, as in John's first letter, fosters a loving
people. The fact that our view of God shapes our lives to a great
extent may be one of the reasons Scripture ascribes such importance to seeking to know him.

On the other hand, Scripture, especially the Old Testa-

ment, strictly forbids making images of Yahweh. This applies in
the first place, no doubt, to carved or sculptured forms. Yet the
danger of having intellectual images of God may be far greater
because these tend to confine the Godhead to our mental limits.
Reducing the Almighty to a manageable size or a limited object
is indeed a common but fatal error. This is harmful for, first of
all, it makes us prone to overlook God when he really comes into our lives, as he continually does in many ways. We are just
too intent on our own idea of God. Secondly, it tends to rob him
of his complete otherness and to confine him to the world that is
ours. St. Thomas Aquinas warns us against this temptation: "If
you comprehend him, he is not God." It is in the same vein that
the Zen master will say: "If you meet the Buddha, kill the Buddha", i.e., if you think you have comprehended the Buddha, destroy your comprehension of him. The secret of this mystery is
to acknowledge that "God is always greater." No matter how
great we think him to be, he is always greater. He can never be
possessed in any way. We can only abandon ourselves to him
and let ourselves be possessed by him.

We have made considerable progress in the knowledge of
God when, before we know who he is, we know who he is not
(St. Augustine). There *is* a relationship with God, but it is beyond our understanding. While he is present to us even more
than we are to ourselves, he transcends our thoughts. *The
Cloud of Unknowing* stresses the fact more than once: "God
may well be loved, but not thought" (ch 6) and "Love may reach
up to God himself even in this life, but not knowledge" (ch 8).[3]
Because we are bound to God as to someone unknown, it requires much courage to live this mystery. It can be quite a shock
to realize that we cannot speak properly about God as 'He', but
only respectfully to God as 'You'. A classic hymn ascribed to St.
Gregory of Nazianzus expresses both the bliss and the pain of
this mystery:

> O all-transcendent God
>   what other name describes you?
> what other words can sing your praises?
>   no word at all denotes you.
> What mind can probe your secret?

No mind at all can grasp you.
Alone beyond the power of speech,
    all men can speak of springs from you;
alone beyond the power of thought,
    all men can think of stems from you.
All things proclaim you -
    things that can speak, things that can not.
All things revere you -
    things that have reason, things that have none.
The whole world's longing and pain
    mingle about you.
All things breathe you a prayer,
    a silent hymn of your own composing.
All that exists you uphold,
    all things in concert move to your orders.
You are the end of all that is,
    you are one, you are all;
you are none of the things that are,
    you are not a part and not the whole.
All names are at your disposal;
    how shall I name you, the only unnameable?
What mind's affinities with heaven
    can pierce the veils above the clouds?
Mercy, all-transcendent God,
    what other name describes you?[4]

Though we cannot speak of God in an adequate way, we cannot be silent about him either. Though we know full well that no image does him complete justice, we cannot refrain from using them. Moreover, because he is beyond our understanding, no single image of him is sufficient. A person who has only one image for God is adoring an idol. This is why Scripture itself presents to us many images and names for God. None of them is commensurate; each one is open-ended and leads into others. The images of Shepherd, Father, Life and Love we shall consider in the next four chapters. This will then lead us to the one image of God which *is* fully adequate, Jesus of Nazareth. On him the rest of the book will dwell.

The name Yahweh was revealed to Moses at the burning

bush in the desert. We too must go into a desert of some kind and come to a personal experience in which we realize that God is the only One. Imbued then with this intimate and yet all-surpassing experience, and vibrant with life from the divine well, we will return and fulfill our liberating mission among the people. "Let us not reproach the world, neither the Church nor life itself for hiding God's face from us. Once we really encounter God, we shall learn that he embraces all things unto himself and that nothing can ever separate us from him unless we want it to. Let us therefore discard these kinds of petty excuses."[5]

God being beyond all images, can never be grasped, but he can grasp and totally fascinate us. The saints and mystics reflect this experience. We too may be eager for such an experience. It can make us better and more alive Christians. Yet a word of caution is in order.[6] Both in our relationships with one another and with God there is a difference between seeking a person, be it God or a human being, and seeking our own experience of that person. Do we seek the person we love in his or her uniqueness of feelings, thoughts, longings and being? Or do we seek an enamored experience of that person? Do we seek the person we appreciate, or do we seek merely the presence we enjoy? Do we seek God or our own spiritual comfort and devotion? It is one thing to be intent on the well-being of the other person; it is quite another thing to try to escape our personal loneliness. As soon as our attention shifts away from the other person and begins to focus on our own experience of that person, we are no longer sincere. St. Augustine called the experience 'amabam amare', i. e., 'I loved to be in love'. It is only through his conversion that his eyes were opened to see the shallowness of what he used to call 'love'!

To seek the experience for experience's sake is to seek self. Many human relationships break down because we forget or perhaps have never known this subtle, basic truth. In many of us the search for God ebbs as the felt experience of his presence is gone. Some 'spiritual' writings deal more with our psychology than with the reality of God, more with our emotional feelings than with the Person of Jesus Christ. Some Christians maintain that "it is my faith that prompts me to act or speak this way." In reality they act or speak according to the dictates of their own principles and ingrained traditions. One can only hope that these are expressions of their faith.

Faith deals with that which is *beyond* expression and experience. Our understanding and the images we use always fall short of the divine reality. Our life pilgrimage will not bring us to a lasting dwelling place here, but hopefully will purify and deepen our relationship with God. May he give us enough generosity and stamina to continue the journey till death do us unite.

> God, this name we call you by
> has become stale.
> It has lost its vigor and its challenge,
> its security and its depth.
> We ask you to reveal once again its meaning
> to our generation.
> Lead us on this lifelong pilgrimage
> wherein your name is spelled out to us
> in a living way.
> Since we will never be able to grasp you,
> we beg you to grasp us
> and to enfold us into the mystery of yourself.
> Give us enough faith
> to always find new life in you,
> and enough openness
> to share it with others
> today and every day, for ever and ever. Amen.

TWO

THE LORD IS MY SHEPHERD

Shepherds play an important role in the Old Testament. Unique in character, they are fequently used as an image for God. The Semitic term expresses well the dynamic lifestyle of the nomadic Jews. They were from the beginning a people always on the move. The nomadic way of life is a vulnerable one. Exposed to dangers of weather and wild animals, the early Hebrews had to be constantly alert and prepared. This natural kind of vigilance in everyday life had a profound influence on the character of the people. When the Jews later became settled and agricultural, they offered the harvest's first fruits in a ceremony that began with the words, "My father was a wandering Aramean..." (Dt 26:5). The words of the prayer kept the original tradition of their wandering ancestors alive.

That the Jewish nation was originally a shepherd people becomes clear when we consider some of the great figures of their history. There is first of all Abraham, father of the chosen nation. He was a royal shepherd with flocks so numerous that the land was not sufficient to accommodate both his herds and those of his cousin Lot. There is Moses, the lawgiver and father of the country. He was tending his father-in-law Jethro's sheep when Jahweh appeared to him in the burning bush and commissioned him to deliver the people of Israel from Egypt. As a guarantee for that mission, Yahweh revealed his name to

CERTAIN AS THE DAWN

Moses. Finally there is David, founder of the dynasty from which the Messiah is to be born. He was tending his father's sheep when Samuel arrived in Bethlehem to anoint one of Jesse's sons to succeed Saul as king of Israel. When the father had proudly presented seven of his sons as possible candidates, the high priest still was not satisfied. Upon inquiry Jesse answered: "There is still the youngest, who is tending the sheep" (1 Sm 16:11). Then David was called from the pastures and Samuel anointed the young shepherd without delay before his father and all his brothers. Thus Psalm 78 can rightly say:

> He chose David, his servant,
> and took him from the sheepfolds;
> from following the ewes he brought him
> to shepherd Jacob, his people,
> and Israel, his inheritance.
> And he tended them with a sincere heart,
> and with skillful hands he guided them (v 70-71).

It seems therefore that the leaders of Jewish history, as well as the people they governed, were shepherds. Since this profession is rare now in western countries and differs considerably from the original Semitic tradition, it may be well to investigate a little more the concept of the Old Testament shepherd.

In Hebrew there are three different synonyms for the word 'shepherd'. This is not surprising for the greater the role a concept plays in the life of a people, the greater the number of interpretations. Thus we are told that the Eskimos have fifteen distinct words for snow. Some African tribes have twenty various names for what we call bananas. And the Indonesian has five different words for the succeeding growth stages of rice.

Though the three Hebrew synonyms for the word 'shepherd' have basically the same meaning, each has its own special connotation. Thus we find within the term: to observe keenly, to watch with utmost attention; to be habitually on one's guard, alerted to and prepared for imminent danger; and to analyze, look ahead and plan. The active dimension of all three words make each more verb than noun.

This etymological approach teaches us that a shepherd is one who embodies all three connotations. He is wide awake, vigilant, watchful, ready, caring and careful. A few years ago I met some Flemish teenagers who had hiked through a part of France. They told me that one morning they had met a shepherd with his flock and had decided to spend the day with him and his sheep. At the end of the day the young people could not help but marvel that the shepherd had not sat down during the entire day. He would lean on his stick occasionally, but would never sit lest he lose sight of his herd.

A shepherd is a dedicated person. There is something of a mystique about a shepherd who lives with and for his flock. A beautiful expression of this mentality is found in Nathan's little parable which he uses to open the eyes of King David after his affair with Bathsheba. The prophet tells about a poor man who had a little ewe lamb: "He nourished her, and she grew up with him and his children. She shared the little food he had and drank from his cup and slept in his bosom. She was like a daughter to him" (2 Sm 12:3). A missionary among the shepherds of the Beka-plain in Lebanon told me that many of his people literally sleep with their animals and...that one can smell it! It is in this way that the shepherd knows his animals and that they know him. He lives so close to them that he can feel and sense how they are. No change or want ever escapes his attention. His authority with his sheep is based completely on his steady presence, dedication and care.

A shepherd is by no means a weakling; he is a man capable and willing to defend his animals even to the point of a bloody fight. Here again David provides a typical example as recorded in 1 Sm 17. David's father had sent his son to the army camp to bring extra food to his three brothers who were at war against the Philistines. There David saw how Goliath challenged the Israeli army by summoning any one of them to a single combat. David, shocked that no one was courageous enough to accept the challenge, immediately offered himself for the fight. King Saul tried to dissuade him because David was only a youth and by no means strong enough to fight the giant. David responded, "Your servant used to tend his father's sheep, and whenever a lion or a bear came to carry off a sheep from the flock, I would go after it and attack it and rescue the prey from its mouth. If it attacked me, I would seize it by the jaw, strike it, and kill it. Your servant has killed both a lion and a bear, and this uncircumcised Philistine will be as one of them, because he has insulted the armies of the living God" (34-36). The example says something about the courage of a shepherd boy.

Dedicated and courageous, a shepherd is also a man with economic responsibility. In those days bank notes and stocks did not exist. Capital was largely invested in herds entrusted to a shepherd. When sheep were lost, he was called to account and to restitution. This dependability and sense of responsibility is also a trait of the good shepherd Jesus. We hear him say, "It is the will of him who sent me that I should lose nothing of what he has given me" (Jn 6:39), and again at the end of his life, "As long as I was with them, I guarded them with your name which you gave me. I kept careful watch, and not one of them was lost, none but him who was destined to be lost -- in fulfillment of Scripture" (Jn 17:12).

By contrast, a bad shepherd is a real disgrace. Many Old Testament passages express vehemently the condemnation of a failing shepherd:

> Therefore, shepherds, hear the word of the Lord:
> As I live, says the Lord God, because my sheep have
> been given over to pillage, and because my sheep
> have become food for every wild beast, for lack of a
> shepherd; because my shepherds did not look after
> my sheep, but pastured themselves and did not
> pasture my sheep; because of this, shepherds, hear
> the word of the Lord: Thus says the Lord God: I
> swear I am coming against these shepherds. I will
> claim my sheep from them and put a stop to their
> shepherding my sheep so that they may no longer
> pasture themselves. I will save my sheep, that they
> may no longer be food for their mouths (Ez 34:7-10).
> Woe to the shepherds who mislead and scatter the
> flock of my pasture, says the Lord. Therefore, thus
> says the Lord, the God of Israel, against the

shepherds who shepherd my people: You have scattered my sheep and driven them away. You have not cared for them, but I will take care to punish your evil deeds (Jer 23:1-2).

My wrath is kindled against the shepherds, and I will punish the leaders (Zec 10:3).

The harsh words about bad shepherds bring out in a negative way the esteem for good shepherds.

*****

In a people with such a glorious tradition of shepherding, one can expect that the image of a shepherd be used as an image for their God. Numerous are the examples where Yahweh is described as a shepherd. "The Lord is my shepherd; I shall not want" (Ps 23:1, the psalm Emmanuel Kant said gave him more consolation than all the books he had ever read). "O shepherd of Israel, hearken, O guide of the flock of Joseph!" (Ps 80:2). "For he is our God, and we are the people he shepherds, the flock he guides" (Ps 95:7). "Here comes with power the Lord God...Like a shepherd he feeds his flock; in his arms he gathers the lambs, carrying them in his bosom, and leading the ewes with care" (Is 40:10-11).

Using the shepherd image for their God, the chosen people envisioned Yahweh with characteristics that stem from their experience. This distinguishes their concept of God from that of surrounding peoples. The most important of these unique traits is the active presence of Yahweh among them. This concept eventually evolves into the idea of God's omnipresence, an attribute typical of the religions of Jewish origin. In old Oriental nature religions the static god resided in his temple from which he exercised his influence. There he was met; there he received the sacrifices offered to him. When the worshipper left the temple, the god remained. Yahweh is different; he goes with his people. "I will set my dwelling among you, and will not disdain you. Ever present in your midst, I will be your God, and you will be my people" (Lv 26:11-12).

The name Yahweh, revealed to Moses from the burning bush, is a mysterious name. It does not give away its secret. Perhaps that is why it could be revealed at all. Shelves of books have been written speculating on the meaning of those four Hebrew Letters. One thing is sure: the name is to be understood in an existential way rather than as a philosophical notion of essence in itself. The Jewish scholar Martin Buber suggests the meaning "I am where you are", or "I am there". It expresses an effective presence that is completely open and uncircumscribed. Yet this presence is strongly affirmative, confirming, giving a sense of security. If Buber is right, the name Emmanuel would be perfectly in line with the name Yahweh. The conclusion of Matthew's Gospel would then be a further elaboration of the Old Testament's interpretation of the 'Name'. "Know that I am with you always, until the end of the world!" (28:20).

The Israelite idea of God is a dynamic relationship. Yahweh is met, experienced wherever one goes. Psalm 139 expresses this nearness in a classic way:

> Where can I go from your spirit?
> from your presence where can I flee?
> If I go up to the heavens, you are there;
> if I sink to the nether world, you are present there.
> If I take the wings of the dawn,
> if I settle at the farthest limits of the sea,
> Even there your hand shall guide me,
> and your right hand hold me fast.
> If I say, "surely the darkness shall hide me,
> and night shall be my light"
> For you darkness itself is not dark,
> and night shines as the day (v 7-12).

This is not just theory; rather it is a faith experience. The people have known Yahweh as a shepherd. They have experienced his reliability in the past and therefore have faith in the future. His faithfulness is a rock on which they can build a life. This gives them a sense of security. There is a magnificent psalm in which the word 'shepherd' does not even occur; yet it could never have been conceived except in a nation thoroughly familiar with the idea that God is like a shepherd.

> I lift up my eyes toward the mountains;
>   whence shall help come to me?
> My help is from the Lord,
>   who made heaven and earth.
>
> May he not suffer your foot to slip;
>   may he slumber not who guards you:
> Indeed he neither slumbers nor sleeps,
>   the guardian of Israel.
>
> The Lord is your guardian; the Lord is your shade;
>   he is beside you at your right hand.
> The sun shall not harm you by day,
>   nor the moon by night.
>
> The Lord will guard you from all evil;
>   he will guard your life.
> The Lord will guard your coming and your going,
>   both now and forever (Ps 121).

It is on these convictions that Israel lived. Their religion was not an abstract one; rather it was a living human experience of the divine reality, a reality so profound and strong that it proved to be the cornerstone for the Jewish nation. To confess God was to tell a story, to expound its meaning and to share it from generation to generation.

*****

The shepherd concept comes full circle. Raised to the level of the divine, the notion of a human shepherd is applied to God. He in turn, calls people to be shepherds in his name and thus the circle becomes complete. First the Messiah, the son of David, pastures the flock. Later others take up the task of Jesus and continue his mission.

In Ezekiel 34 all aspects of the shepherd come together. "I mean to raise up one shepherd, my servant David, and to put him in charge of them and he will shepherd them; he will pasture them and be their shepherd. I, Yahweh, will be their God, and my servant David shall be their ruler" (v 23, JB). The next seven verses, using the image of the shepherd, explain the work of the Messiah who tends the flock for Yahweh. To the present day this passage sets the standard for all pastoral service.

In the New Testament, especially in John 10, Jesus applies the image of the good shepherd to himself. This was a favorite of the early Christians. What the crucifix is in our day, the figure of the good shepherd was in the early Church. The many pictures and sculptures of the good shepherd in the catacombs confirm the fact. In comparison the oldest crucifix dates only from the fifth century.[1] We have become so used to the image of the crucified Lord that we fail to realize how shocking a crucifix would have been to the early Christians. We easily restrict ourselves to the artistic approach of the crucifix and hardly comprehend the terrible reality behind it. There is a Dutch saying: "In the house of the man who was hanged, one does not speak of the gallows." The early Church had a similar sensitivity which partially explains why it took so long for the crucifix to appear in Christian art. They held dearly to the richness of the good shepherd image.

In describing himself as the good shepherd, Jesus reveals much about himself and about his Father. He makes it clear from the beginning that God's presence as shepherd is not general or impersonal. It is individual and very personal. "He calls his own by name" (v 3), and "he walks in front of them, and the sheep follow him, because they recognize his voice" (v 4), and also "I know my sheep and my sheep know me in the same way that the Father knows me and I know the Father" (v 14-15). The comparison refers to a practice in the time of Jesus. Several herds were sheltered for the night in the same compound; at dawn each shepherd would call his own sheep. They, recognizing their master's voice, would follow him to pasture. The mutual recognition of sheep and shepherd is so significant that Jesus likens it to his intimate relationship with his Father. Within the reach of the good shepherd's voice there is shalom: safety, shelter and food.

The same personal concern is seen in the parable of the lost sheep. The shepherd leaves the ninety-nine in the wasteland to search for the lost one (Lk 15:3-7). In Mk 6:34 Jesus takes pity on the crowd and feeds them. But he does even more. In total giving Jesus pays the price for true shepherding. He gives his life for his sheep by living for them, dying for them and even feeding them with his own flesh. Thus, Psalm 23 which says, "You spread the table before me...my cup overflows" (v 5) is fulfilled in a pointed way. In a mysterious paradox the shepherd has to become a lamb. This reversal has overtones of being led to the slaughter and not opening his mouth. "The lamb on the throne will shepherd them. He will lead them to springs of life-giving water, and God will wipe every tear from their eyes" (Rv. 7:17).

It is not only the Messiah who is to shepherd the flock in Yahweh's name. Others are to share this mission. "I will appoint over you shepherds after my own heart, who will shepherd you wisely and prudently" (Jer 3:15). God needs men and women to look after his people. We are to incarnate his life and his love, his care and his concern. We are his chosen servants who act in his name and in his way. We are commissioned by God himself. The roots of our mission, based on the needs of the people, go deep and are of divine origin. Peter describes this pastoral task:

> God's flock is in your midst; give it a shepherd's care. Watch over it willingly as God would have you do, not under constraint; and not for shameful profit either, but generously. Be examples to the flock, not lording it over those assigned to you, so that when the chief Shepherd appears you will win for yourselves the unfading crown of glory (1 Pt 5:2-4).

Care and concern, Peter insists, are not enough. As true shepherds, we need to have respect for those we serve. Respect is the heart of love. How could we continue the task of the chief Shepherd when respect is lacking?

The New Testament also reinforces the need for a strong sense of responsibility, a characteristic so prominent in the Old Testament shepherd. We find an example in Paul's farewell address to the elders of Miletus:

> Keep watch over yourselves, and over the whole flock the Holy Spirit has given you to guard. Shepherd the church of God, which he has acquired at the price of his own blood. I know that when I am gone, savage wolves will come among you who will not spare the flock. From your own number, men will present themselves distorting the truth and leading astray any who follow them. Be on guard, therefore. Do not forget that for three years, night and day, I never ceased warning you individually even to the point of tears (Acts 20:28-31).

Faith in God is to accept his shepherd's care. Growth in faith is to become imbued with his care. Mature faith is to share his care for others.

> Almighty God,
> you are the shepherd with whom all creatures are safe.
> You watch over us with gentle care.
> You are always present to us
> in an active, loving way.
> You have given us your Son,
> so that your concern for us might be visible and tangible.
> He went so far as to lay down his life for us;
> as a lamb he was led to the slaughter.
> We ask of you the grace
> to be completely secure in your protection,
> and to experience always that deep peace
> which the world can neither give nor take away.
> We also ask you
> that we in our turn shepherd in love
> those you have entrusted to us,
> so that your kingdom may grow,
> today and every day, for ever and ever. Amen.

THREE

OUR FATHER IN HEAVEN

The favorite image of God in the New Testament is that of Father. Jesus himself refers to God almost exclusively in that way. Consequently we are all quite familiar with this concept. Yet the true biblical meaning of the image may elude us. This is due in part to the decline of fatherhood in our society. Almost twenty years ago Alexander Mitscherlich wrote his famous book *Society without the Father*.[1] In it the author gives a description and an interpretation of the trends toward a fatherless society in the western world. This movement became more marked as time went on, so that fifteen years later Lance Morrow could write: "Of the 50,000 parents who responded to a query by Advice Columnist Ann Landers, a depressing 70% said that given the choice again, they would not have children: it wasn't worth it."[2]

This recent depreciation of parenthood is one reason for today's world failing to understand the scriptural term father. Prior to this there already developed a tremendous gap between the father concept of modern times and the father pattern of the biblical world. People today tend to think that the word father has the same meaning now as it did in Jesus' time. However, the role of father for Jesus and his contemporaries was far more comprehensive than it is today. In this modern world people grow up in a complicated and specialized society with a variety

of influences outside the home. In Jesus' time, a child was dependent almost solely on his father and mother. Of necessity there generated an intimacy between father and child - a bond, strong and all-encompassing, uncommon in our day.

In the light of this historical-sociological background, we must keep in mind the two essential aspects of the Scriptural meaning of the word father. First of all it means lord and ruler, full control and authority. Secondly, it means care, concern and reliability. Whenever the term is used, although the emphasis may vary, these two strands of meaning interweave.

In the Old Testament there are a few texts which call God Father. The earlier references show God as Father of the people as a whole; only in more recent books of the Old Testament God is mentioned as Father of the individual.

Some examples of the earlier approaches which stress the authority aspect are:
-certain lines from the song in which Moses summarizes the history of Yahweh with his people:

> Is the Lord to be thus repaid by you,
>   O stupid and foolish people?
> Is he not your father who created you?...
> You were unmindful of the Rock that begot you,
>   you forgot the God who gave you birth.
> When the Lord saw this, he was filled with loathing
>   and anger toward his sons and daughters (Dt 32:6, 18-19).

-a few lines from the great psalm in which a disciple of the prophet Isaiah towards the end of the Babylonian Exile recalls God's goodness: "O Lord, you are our father; we are the clay and you the potter: we are all the work of your hands" (Is 64:7).

The mercy and care of Yahweh for his people are also emphasized:
-In the same passage of Isaiah we read:

> Look down from heaven and regard us
>   from your holy and glorious palace!
> Where is your zealous care and your might,

your surge of pity and your mercy?
O Lord, hold not back, for you are our father.
Were Abraham not to know us,
    nor Israel to acknowledge us,
You, Lord, are our father,
    our redeemer you are named forever (Is 63:15-16).

-A particularly tender passage is found in chapter 11 of the prophet Hosea:

When Israel was a child I loved him,
    out of Egypt I called my son...
It was I who taught Ephraim to walk,
    who took them in my arms;
I drew them with human cords,
    with bands of love;
I fostered them like one
    who raises an infant to his cheeks;...
My heart is overwhelmed,
    my pity is stirred.
I will not give vent to my blazing anger,
    I will not destroy Ephraim again;
For I am God and not man,
    the Holy One present among you (v 1-9 passim).

We find God as father of the individual for the first time in the Lord's promises to David:
-"I will be a father to him, and he shall be a son to me" (2 Sm 7:14).
-"He shall say of me, 'You are my father, my God, the Rock, my savior'.
...Forever I will maintain my kindness toward him, and my covenant with him stands firm" (Ps 89:27-29).

Towards the end of the Old Testament the individual has come to address God as father:
-"Lord, Father and Master of my life, permit me not to fall by them!" (Sir 23:1).
-"Lord, Father and God of my life, abandon me not into their control!" (Sir 23:4).

-"I called out: O Lord, you are my father, you are my champion and my savior; do not abandon me in time of trouble, in the midst of storms and dangers" (Sir 51:10).

*****

Scarce in the Old Testament, New Testament instances of God as Father abound. Jesus constantly refers to God as his Father. In the sixth chapter of Matthew alone, Jesus calls God his Father twelve times; in the four Gospels together the term occurs 177 times. It is the first and the last recorded word of Jesus in Luke's Gospel. He is twelve years old when we hear him say: "Did you not know I had to be in my Father's house?" (2:49). Shortly before he died he spoke his last word, "Father, into your hands I commend my spirit" (23:46). In between, the gospels cite numerous other occasions when Jesus turned to his Father.

Son in a unique sense, Jesus does not keep this privilege for himself. By teaching us to relate to God as he does, he shares the intimacy with us. In this sharing lies an exclusive part of his mission. In his farewell discourse he states, "No one comes to the Father but through me" (Jn 14:6). Surely there are many who come to God without knowing Jesus. One has only to think of great world religions like Hinduism and Buddhism. How generous and sincere many times are their efforts in their search for God. How profound and even mystical their experiences! Yet in spite of their immeasurable spiritual depth, they seldom or never come to God as father. Indeed the approach to divine fatherhood is one of the greatest treasures Jesus brought us.

In Jesus' living as Son we find both aspects of the scriptural meaning of the word 'father'. For Jesus too, the Father is ruler and lord: "Father, Lord of heaven and earth, to you I offer praise" (Mt. 11:25). Because of his lordship, God is to be obeyed: "Doing the will of him who sent me and bringing his work to completion is my food" (Jn 4:34) and "I always do what pleases him" (Jn 8:29). However the other aspect is also present in an extraordinary degree of trust and intimacy. This leads Jesus to address his Father with the tender, affectionate word 'Abba'. The overtones of this small word will always remain beyond us. Yet we sense in it something of the closeness of Jesus with his Father. We touch in it the very heart of his personality. This Abba relationship made him the person he was. It freed him from all self-concern and enabled him to relate to each and every person with great ease, openness, sympathy and a liberating love.[3]

We too are not only invited but also called to enter into this warm and liberating experience with the Father. St. Paul is most explicit about it, "All who are led by the Spirit of God are sons of God. You did not receive a spirit of slavery leading you back into fear, but a spirit of adoption through which we cry out, 'Abba!' (that is 'Father')" (Rm 8:14-15). Fear, both of the past and of the future, can do much harm. On the one hand, it can make us defensive, closed to any progress, or on the other hand, it can make us rush forward for fear of not being 'with it'. Fear can cause uncharitableness towards others and phariseeism in our relation to God. It can stifle the best in us. All we do under the impulse of it does not bear the fruits of the Spirit. The deep-rooted realization that God is our Abba will drive out fear. A new freedom then blossoms, that same freedom that made Jesus so attractive and authentic. We are privileged to share in the intimacy of Jesus with his Father. The Son wants to glorify his Father in us by the way we live. He wants something of the Father's radiance and fulness of life to shine forth. The Father in his turn wants to glorify his Son in us so that the spirit of Jesus lives on. We become an incarnation in which the mystery of the Son is renewed.

John no less than Paul is enthusiastic about our Abba relationship. "See what love the Father has bestowed on us in letting us be called children of God! Yet that is what we are" (1 Jn 3:1). It is the key effect of the incarnation and the culmination of his Gospel's prologue: "Any who did accept him he empowered to become children of God" (Jn 1:12).

In response, God's fatherhood implies that man obey his will. For Jesus this was his food; he demands the same from all who follow him. It is the touchstone for the authenticity of our belief in the Father. "None of those who cry out, 'Lord, Lord,' will enter the kingdom of God but only the one who does the will of my Father in heaven" (Mt 7:21). "Whoever does the will

of my heavenly Father is brother and sister and mother to me"
(Mt 12:50).

That God is Father is the Good News Jesus wants to bring
home to us. To believe this, not just with the head but also with
the heart, makes all the difference.

*****

In our experience of fatherhood we find the qualities of initiative, loves, care, space, roots, forgiveness and universality.
The father takes *initiative*. Every father is creative in begetting
life. He loves the child even before his or her birth. Thus St. Augustine can say, "You created me, because you loved me." Indeed, the heavenly Father does not start loving his child after or
even while he creates him, but his love is the origin of his being
created at all. Here we touch the liberating truth of the 'prior
love', which deeply inspired St. Bernard and of which John says
in his first letter, "Love, then, consists in this: not that we have
loved God but that he has loved us" (4:10). A father gives freely.
His love is based on nothing. He takes risks in procreating. No
one can guarantee that the child will be sound physically, men-
tally or morally. The only thing a father can do is love his child
into goodness. Such is the role of our heavenly Father.

Fatherhood implies *love*. It means tenderness and warmth,
kindness, reliability and concern. "Can a mother forget her in-
fant, be without tenderness for the child of her womb? Even
should she forget, I will never forget you" (Is 49:15). Though a
child obviously depends on his father, the reverse is also true.
The happiness of a father is either greatly enhanced or frustrated by what the child becomes for the parent is bonded to the
child. Love makes us vulnerable; true fatherhood means growth
in unselfishness. Has man failed, perhaps, to apply this principle to God and in consequence made God into something of a
caricature of a father? Has the Christian been too much in-
fluenced by the philosophy of Aristotle who called God 'the unmoved all-mover' and thus portrayed him as absolutely aloof
and unconcerned? Has not the French encyclopedist Diderot a
point in his cutting remark: "There is no good father who would
want to be like our heavenly Father"?

Flowing from a father's love is his *care*. It prompts Peter to give this advice, "Cast all your cares on God because he cares for you" (1 Pt 5:7). This realization will free us from undue worries. Jesus stresses it even more: "If you, with all your sins, know how to give your children what is good, how much more will your heavenly Father give good things to anyone who asks him!" (Mt 7:11). "Are not two sparrows sold for next to nothing? Yet not a single sparrow falls to the ground without your Father's consent. As for you, every hair of your head has been counted; so do not be afraid of anything. You are worth more than an entire flock of sparrows" (Mt 10:29-31).

A father *provides space* for his child to become himself. While thus providing the security and challenge in which autonomous life can develop, the father affirms the child's individuality. He gives the child a name. This makes it possible to address the child and enables the child to respond as a person. The name given the child brings identity and calls forth responsibility. Similarly the heavenly Father has called each of us by name. Jesus adds, "It is to the glory of my Father that you should bear much fruit, and then you will be my disciples" (Jn 15:8 JB).

To my father I owe my *roots*. Thousands of generations of ancestors have lived and died, but when my father dies, I am an orphan. It is through my father that I am rooted in my forefathers. We need these roots more now than ever before. We often say that through TV our world becomes a small world. The opposite however is also true; our living room becomes so large that we are never at home. The Bible sets aside a cozy 4,000 years for the human history B.C. For us it has become billions of years in which our lifetime is lost as a microscopic fragment. A sense of uprootedness can make us restless and oppressed. When we call God Father we think primarily of his goodness and concern; however, there is much more involved - namely, security, basic trust and roots. "...rooted in love and built on love" (Eph 3:17). Freud considered the belief in God as an immature prolongation of the relationship with our father. But could it not be the other way around? Could not the relationship with our father be rooted in an earlier and deeper relation to God the Father? "That is why I kneel before the Father from whom every family in heaven and on earth takes its name" (Eph 3:14-15). To shift the imagery somewhat: our relation to God as Father is the anchor in the deepest Ground of our being.

In the Biblical message the father *forgives*. The most beautiful attempt of Jesus to picture his Father is the parable of the prodigal son. The love of the father for the son is so unselfish and so pure that there is no semblance of wounded pride or egoistic bitterness in his heart. He can embrace his runaway boy without reproach and in doing so brings him back to life. "...this son of mine was dead and has come back to life" (Lk 15:24). The father having given life once, can also restore it. The awareness that the father is able to bring back life is an essential implication of Christ's message. Father stands for a new dawn.

Universality is another characteristic of the divine fatherhood. He causes his sun to rise on the bad as well as on the good, and his rain to fall on the just and on the unjust alike (Mt 5:45). He is Father of us all and he wants us to live as brothers and sisters of one family. Indeed, we are brothers and sisters, but not on the romantic basis of Beethoven's '*Alle Menschen werden Brüder*' - 'All People Will Become Brothers', nor on the abstract foundation of a human ideology. Neither is our relationship by blood or urge of the flesh; it is rather a divine reality. Compared to the Old Testament, the New evokes a greater intimacy with God. This in turn establishes a greater universality and a stronger union between all people. Where faith in God's fatherhood is alive, the oneness among all God's people becomes stronger. Charity and unity are *the* signs that render our faith credible and real.

As this chapter closes, it seems important to comment on a relevant and delicate topic. Having dealt with the scriptural, literal and connotative meanings of the word father, what about a presentation of this nature to a person whose childhood experiences of his father have not been that positive? In fact, whenever one speaks to an audience about God as Father, one can tell that some of the people become uneasy; it is not hard to understand why. The best advice in this predicament, it seems to me, was given by Viktor E. Frankl. He points out:

A pan-deterministic evaluation of religion contends

that one's religious life is conditioned inasmuch as it depends on one's early childhood experiences, and that one's God concept depends on one's father image. In contrast to this view, it is well known that the son of a drunkard need not become a drunkard himself; and in the same manner, a man may resist the detrimental influence of a dreadful father image and establish a sound relationship with God. Even the worst father image need not prevent one from establishing a good relationship with God; rather, a deep religious life provides one with the resources needed to overcome the hatred of one's father. Conversely, a poor religious life need not in each case be due to developmental factors.

He confirms this remark from a broad experience:

A cross-sectional statistical survey conducted by my staff at the Vienna Poliklinik Hospital revealed that about one-third of those patients who had experienced a positive father image turned away from religion in their later life, whereas most of those people screened who had a negative father image succeeded, in spite of this, in building up a positive attitude toward religious issues.[4]

God of all ages,
Jesus of Nazareth shared with us
your name 'Father'.
He revealed to us
how he owed his whole being to you,
and how the secret of his life
was his oneness with you.
Through him you have become
accessible and fascinating to us.
We now know you to be
not merely the source of our existence
but a caring, loving Father
on whom we can completely depend.

We ask you,
may we always respectfully receive your Name from
him,
genuinely keep it alive among us,
and faithfully pass it on to others,
today and every day for ever and ever. Amen.

FOUR

GIVER OF LIFE

Feast Without End. This title of a diary by Roger Schutz, prior of Taizé, suggests a remarkably happy man. When asked, "What makes your life a feast, Frère Roger?" he answered, "First of all accepting myself as I am." To accept oneself as one is then marks the beginning of the feast without end. This is difficult, however, and it is rare.

Few people love themselves

For many people the idea of loving themselves seems like a temptation - almost a sacrilege. They have not yet discovered the difference between the negative self-love and the good and God-willed love of self. Quite a few well-versed in Catholic doctrine think that it is a part of our faith content to understand humankind as basically evil because of original sin. Some Catholics not only think that way but they also live that way. The effects of this misconception stamp their very lives. In spiritual counseling and direction the basic problem is often a negative self-concept, a low level of confidence, an inability to appreciate the value of self, and a lack of self-acceptance. All contribute to making a person miserable. Many good Christians have difficulty owning the good that is in them. When questioned about it they, somewhat aghast, admit that they have never given it much thought. This means, of course, that they never thanked God much for it either. Mary gives us a different example in her 'Magnificat'. She does not belittle the things done to her, but calls them great. Psalm 103 also teaches us to forget none of all God's benefits. It would be well for us occasionally to stage a talent-search instead of a fault-finding - and to count our blessings!

In our training, our negative qualities were perhaps emphasized too much. No doubt this happened with the best of intentions: either it was meant to jolt some into an awareness of their faults in order to outgrow them or to prevent self-complacency and pride. Pushed too far at times, it ceased being lifegiving. Often it resulted in a self-defensive stance, a tendency towards an inferiority complex, an escape into a playing games and wearing a mask, a continuous comparing with others, a competitive lifestyle and a heightened tendency towards jealousy.

Many people feel threatened by their peers

To experience another person as a competitor or as a threat is quite common. When my faith in my self is weak, I want to assert myself. I need to prove to others and to myself that I am worthwhile after all. Often enough an excessive tendency towards competition turns everyone else into a rival. A tragic situation then evolves: someone else is praised -- I with my poor self-concept feel attacked. I create competition even though it is not a win-lose situation at all.

To cite another example: a young man having suffered rejection at one time generalizes the particular experience. He convinces himself first that nobody cares for him and later that he is not worth caring about. He fails to pick up the signals of affection transmitted to him because his negative view filters them out. When others begin indeed to show him less signs of recognition, his prophecy has fulfilled itself.

To dislike another does not usually mean to love myself too much; rather it means that I love myself too little. I dislike the other because I do not really like myself. When I do not love myself I can hardly expect to be loved by others. In fact, I may tend to consider myself as basically unlovable by everyone. I may become suspicious, defensive, perhaps even aggressive. I cannot afford to face, let alone admit, my own shortcomings. The negative in me, my shadow as Jung would call it, is repressed because I fail to acknowledge sufficiently the good in me. In either dimension, my self-concept is not realistic enough. My tense and uptight defensiveness hardly allows for a real growth and fulfillment.

Many people are lonely

We have all heard about the terrible loneliness of many elderly people; some even die so alone that they are found only days later. The young generation wrestles no less and perhaps even more with poignant feelings of loneliness. It becomes a disease and brings immense suffering. Many in middle-age suffer from isolation in their mid-life crisis.

The fear of loneliness is often more disconcerting than loneliness itself. Many of us fail to be aware of the 'true presence' of another. The person who accepts me as I am and is faithful and reliable in that acceptance and whose support I know to be there, he or she is truly present. But in many lives there is no such presence. A desperate and almost compulsive urge to verify that 'true presence' often stifles the little of it there is. Some crave a deep, personal relationship so eagerly that they crush it in bud. We sometimes tend to make excessive demands on those we call friends. Thus we prepare the way for bitterness and hostility when these 'friends' fail to live up to our unrealistic expectations. All this causes deep suffering and can even create despair which renders everything, including life itself, meaningless. Underneath affectation can lie feelings of lonesomeness and worthlessness.

Many people are not at home with themselves

If we are not at home with ourselves, we will never be at home with anyone else. We may try to escape in activism. This is, of course, equivalent to yielding to the problem and making it insoluble. When I was young, I used to look up with awe at the motorcycle riders who at my hometown's annual fun fair rode the steep wall. To have enough speed was the trick. If the riders were to go slowly, they would drop to the floor in the middle of the tent. Later I discerned in this act an image of how some of us live; the whole secret again is speed. Whenever we slow down, we drop into the big hole in the middle of our lives. We are like a wood shaving curled around its own emptiness. We create so much busyness and convince ourselves so deeply of its utter necessity that no time is left to confront ourselves in our basic loneliness and emptiness.

Consumerism can be another attempt to escape or to fill up the gap created by loneliness. We try to heal temporarily the frustration of an unfulfilled dream by amassing material possessions. But alas, these acquisitions are like salt water - the more we drink of it, the more parching our thirst becomes. Since we pamper ourselves so well, we may give the impression that we really do love ourselves. Yet deep down we all realize that this behavior is in fact, a coverup for a lack of love.

When there is too little love, things become enormously important - to the point of addiction. Food and drink, likes and dislikes, enjoyment, possessions, work, status, influence, recognition and a host of other substitutes take on great value. To the degree that love decreases, the want for everything that is not love increases.

The craving for life's meaningfulness, the intuition where it is to be found and the awareness of its fragility are tersely expressed by Jean-Paul Sartre: "The peak of love's joy, if it exists at all, is to feel that life is worth living."

*****

André Gide observed that people are extremely clever in preventing their being happy - happiness understood in its broad and deeply fulfilling meaning. Indeed this sort of happiness is a much neglected mission. Faith is a basic aid in this mission, since faith is all about love, and since only love can achieve life's justification and happiness. We all carry in ourselves many possibilities as the buds contain the foliage and flowers to be. First, however, they have to open up and that will happen only in the appropriate climate. As long as the weather is bleak and cold, they remain closed. When spring comes and the sun shines, they open up and an array of green and flowers emerges. People are like that.

Each of us has a share of priceless abilities in head, heart and hands. There is such a variety of ways in which people are gifted that each of us has great promise in a unique way. Like nature, which is never thrifty or stingy in germinating, every human being has much inherent potential. All this, however, remains hidden as long as the surrounding atmosphere is chilly and adverse. Only in the climate of love can talents begin to blossom and treasures be revealed. "My Father has been glorified in your bearing much fruit..." (Jn 15:8). This is what the Father wants and had in mind when he called us into being; this is the innate aspiration of our very nature.

The value of self may not be constituted by love but certainly only love can bring out this worth. Only in love can we experience the joy of knowing that life is worthwhile, fruitful and justified. The joy of that realization we cannot give to ourselves. It can only be received from others. In the last analysis God himself is the source.

We are speaking here of the love we give to others. People who really love much have no problem with the meaning of life - they live it! "Love and do whatever you want", says St. Augustine. Life will be good! Before we can give love though, we have to receive it. To be loved is more basic than to love. The realization of being loved is the most fundamental yearning of every human heart. In the vein of St. Augustine we could say: "Know yourself loved and do whatever you want." Each of us needs more love than we deserve. That is one reason why it can never be purchased or forced, but only given and received.

Our longing, moreover, is not for a love that is short-lived, conditional or meager. It has to last forever, should have no strings attached and must go to the very end. This means that God alone is the ultimate fulfillment of our desire. Human love can easily manipulate the other person: "if you really loved me, you would not do that..." or "you would do this for me". Only God's love has no prerequisites. It is based on nothing, but it is itself the basis of everything. It is sheer surprise. It is bottomless abyss. The fact that it is based on nothing makes us secure. Were it based on anything, and were that 'anything' to collapse, then God's love would crumble as well. But with God no such thing can possibly happen. People who realize this can live freely and to the full. Like Atlas, who carries the whole world, some mistakenly support the enormous burden of trying to deserve God's love. Even the mere watching of this lifestyle is enervating. I would like to say to Atlas, "Put down that globe and dance on it; this is the purpose for which it was made." I want likewise to say to these weary people, "Lay down your load and build your life on God's love; only that kind of living is sound." We do not have to earn God's love; neither do we have to support it. It is free gift. "Come to me, all you who are weary and find life burdensome, and I will refresh you" (Mt 11:28).

God's love is all-inclusive; it has no restrictions. He loves even the sinner. Sin does not keep God from loving us; rather it shows that we do not love God enough. "If we are unfaithful he will still remain faithful, for he cannot deny himself" (2 Tm 2:13). Sin means that I shield myself from that love and wall myself in against it. If I continue to build that wall for a lifetime, it makes a dungeon so massive that I get trapped in it. The tragedy is that outside, the sun of God's love is still shining.

God's love is all-embracing. Everything is contained within the endless realm of his faithfulness. Though suffering and evil are so worldwide that no family, no individual is exempt, yet, God's love is greater and stronger than any evil and envelops all. "Despite the increase of sin, grace has far surpassed it" (Rm 5:20). His love will always have the last word and everything can be regenerated in it and thus become whole and holy. "We know that God makes all things work together for the good of those who have been called according to his decree" (Rm 8:28).

God's love is the origin and the completion of our life. The traditional way to express this is through the concept of creation. In our modern day the word may have lost much of its fascination. To a degree God's love has slipped out of it. It has often been used in a cold rationalistic setting to explain what cannot be explained anyway, or to force us to an all-out service of the Creator. Some may immediately think of the opening lines of *Ignatius' Spiritual Exercises:* "Man is created to praise, reverence and serve God our Lord and by this means to save his soul." This is easily (mis)understood as a radical way to burden us with submission which leaves no leeway whatsoever. Since we are created we are inescapably caught at the very root of our existence, like born slaves. To ignore this principle is to be punished inexorably.

Ignatius' principle is not meant as strangling but as liberating. To focus on God is the only way to come to lasting fulfillment. To praise and serve God is to make life all-around meaningful. This is not an arbitrary obligation which the All-powerful imposes on us. It is the inborn attraction in our nature that draws us toward God. The principle is not authoritatively composed by God, but it pervades our very hearts where we gradually discover it. It is not God who, after having created the universe, on the seventh day commands us to applaud. It is man marveling at creation and its Creator, who cannot help but applauding. The principle does not express an alien and alienating sway, but profound human wisdom. Many positive and negative experiences have gone into it. Since our options are often intricate and ambiguous, it is a help to receive this directive.

The key to the right interpretation is the realization that creating is an act of love. Creation means that God from all eternity has been longing for precisely this unique human being. God's longing at a certain moment was so intense that this particular person came into being, to live a life everlasting. To this creative love our whole being is attuned and it is only by accurately tuning in to this source that the melody of our life will be completely harmonious to the delight of ourselves, our fellow-men and our Creator.

A few thoughts about the word perfection may be helpful. It seems that the word has three different meanings. First of all, it means without flaw or shortcoming. An example may be that of a perfect speaker with a large vocabulary, a good command of grammar, an excellent pronunciation and a clear and powerful diction - nothing is lacking. The word perfection can also be understood in a different way. Take a person who stutters but has learned to live with his handicap. When he has something to say in private or in public, it may not be pleasant either for him or for his listeners, but he will say it anyway. Here perfection is understood on a more profound level; it is the perfection of this broken world. This person has learned to be at peace with his limitations and to make the best of it in a serene way. He has achieved what Roger Schutz means when he speaks about accepting himself as he is with all the harmony and effectiveness that flows from that. Then there is still a third meaning for the word perfection. In the Bible perfection or holiness means above all a special presence of God. Mount Sinai was holy because Yahweh was present there in a unique way. Moses was perfect because God summoned him to an exceptional divine presence. The name Yahweh was holy since it expressed the very presence of the Holy One.

There seems to be a connection between the third and the second meanings. Since God remains faithful and present to us even in our deficiency, we are able to accept ourselves as we are; self-acceptance is an act of faith! God's unconditional acceptance provides us with a peace which the world cannot give and that in turn makes us bear much more fruit than we could bear all by ourselves. The Christian perfection then is not perfectionism. A perfectionist cannot live with flaws; God can. God is the giver of life, not a stifler of it.

> You have mercy on all, because you can do
>   all things;
>   and you overlook the sins of men that
>   they may repent.
> For you love all things that are and loathe
>   nothing that you have made;
>   for what you hated, you would not have fashioned.
> And how could a thing remain, unless you
>   willed it;
>   or be preserved, had it not been called
>   forth by you?
> But you spare all things, because they are yours,
>   O Lord and lover of life,
>   for your imperishable spirit is in all things! (Wis
> 11:23-12:1).

Almighty God,
we are the work of your hands
which you will never abandon.
All our life is your gift;
all your power is in our being.
You spend yourself on each of us.
We thank you that our life is rooted in yours;
we thank you for all the opportunities you give us,

and for the light that shines on our path,
that warms our hearts.
We pray that gratefulness may prompt us
to live life to the full,
to remain always open to your surprising ways,
and to glorify you through the fruits we bear
today and every day, for ever and ever. Amen.

FIVE

GOD IS LOVE

"We believe in love". This favorite quote from John's first letter summarizes unequivocally what Christianity stands for. We hold that love is the ultimate and decisive value of human life. We believe that love can change the world and we try to put it into practice. Yet, something seems to be lacking in this motto. It sounds comparable to a slogan like 'we believe in democracy', or for that matter, 'we believe in Marxism'. In other words, it may shift faith a bit too much into an ideology. The maxim lacks the personal touch we find in John's original expression. When we look in the Bible to see what John really says, we find that the expression is but a partial quote. The complete sentence is, "We have come to know and to believe in the love God has for us" (1 Jn 4:16). Precisely the last four words change this statement from an abstract ideology into a personal relationship. And that makes all the difference.

Indeed we believe that God loves us. This love is the content of our faith. "We have come to know and to believe in the love God has for us" is a true and magnificent summary of our faith. It expresses the one thing in life that constitutes ultimate meaning and the basis for real happiness. To know that one is loved immensely by God himself is the peak. To believe means to realize not just with the head but also with the heart that God loves *me* in a creative, intimate, unique, reliable and respectful way. Creative: out of his love I come forth; through his love I am who I am. Intimate: his love reaches out to the deepest in me - where I am most myself. Unique: his love embraces me as I am, not as I am considered or supposed to be. Reliable: his love for me will never let me down. Respectful: the heart of love is respect; without it love becomes condescending or manipulative.

God calls me by my name. He is concerned about me and fully understands me. He reads my thoughts, my feelings and my longings. He knows my joys and frustrations, my weaknesses and my strengths. He shares my expectations and my memories. He knows me through and through from having watched my bones take shape. He sees me in laughter and in tears, in illness and in health. He listens to my voice, to my breath, to my heartbeat. I do not love myself more than he does. This leads St. Augustine to say that God is more intimate with me than I am with myself. Faith is the awareness of this intimacy.

The two great commandments of the New Testament are: "'You shall love the Lord your God with your whole heart, with your whole soul, and with all your mind. This is the greatest and first commandment. The second is like it: 'You shall love your neighbor as yourself'" (Mt 22:37-39). But before Jesus imposes these two demands, he first shares with us the good news of his Father's love. He does not begin with the comandments; they are only consequences (and necessary ones) of the good news. In fact, Jesus himself never even brings them up. It is only in answer to questions or objections raised by the Pharisees that he states them. They are no doubt important, yet, they do not form the heart of the New Testament.

It reminds me of a little joke referring to one of our professors. He had written a small book with the brief, bold title *God*. Someone quipped to him, "Of course, it is very important to know how Professor Robbers thinks about God, but it is far more important to know how God thinks about Professor Robbers." In adaptation I would like to say to everyone, "Of course, it is very important that you love God, but is it far more important that God loves you." First things first! If we really know ourselves loved by God, sooner or later our spontaneous response will be to love God in return. This is the first command-ment. Furthermore, once we learn to understand that God also accepts every other person as he or she is, we too will begin to accept the other persons as they are. Both commandments flow freely from the faith that we are loved by God. St. Bernard puts it briefly: "Because we are loved, we love; and because we love, we become worthy to be loved more."[1] Indeed, God is love, un-folding into new loves.

The heart of faith is grace, graciousness and transparency. It is neither a teeth-gritting enterprise nor a self-achieved feat. It brings neither condescension towards others nor self-com-placency in ourselves. A touch of lightness and brightness ac-companies it. Surely it is more gift than accomplishment. It presupposes receptiveness rather than grasping. It is a grace. Therefore the words of Paul Tillich apply well here:

> To be struck by grace does not mean...that we sim-ply are making progress in our moral self-control, in our fight against special faults, and in our relation-ships to men and to society. Moral progress may be a fruit of grace, but it is not grace itself, and it can even prevent us from receiving grace...And certain-ly (grace) does *not* happen if we try to force it upon ourselves, just as it shall not happen so long as we think in our self-complacency that we have no need of it. Grace strikes us when we are in great pain and restlessness. It strikes us when we walk through the dark valley of a meaningless and empty life. It strikes us when we feel our separation is deeper than usual, because we violated another life....It strikes us when our disgust for our own being, our indiffer-ence, our weakness, our hostility, and our lack of direction and composure have become intolerable to us. It strikes us when year after year, the longed-for perfection of life does not appear, when the old complusions reign within us as they have for dec-ades, when despair destroys all joy and courage. Sometimes at that moment a wave of light breaks in-to our darkness and it is as though a voice were sav-

ing: "You are accepted. *You are accepted,* accepted
by that which is greater than you, and the name of
which you do not know. Do not ask for the name
now; perhaps you will find it later. Do not try to do
anything now; perhaps later you will do much. Do
not seek for anything; do not perform anything; do
not intend anything. *Simply accept the fact that you
are accepted!"* If that happens to us, we experience
grace. After such an experience we may not be better than before, and we may not believe more than
before. But everything is transformed. In that moment, grace conquers sin, and reconciliation bridges
the gulf of estrangement. And nothing is demanded
of this experience, no religious or moral or intellectual presuppositions, nothing but acceptance.[2]

When this happens to us, we do not have to *do* anything except first let ourselves be imbued with this realization. When
little children are forced to walk too early, they become bow-
legged. In spiritual life there exists a similar phenomenon of doing too much too soon which has lifelong harmful effects. In the
comparison of the true vine Jesus says, "Remain in my love" (Jn
15:9 JB). It is not enough to have touched God's love. We have
to grasp the hand that reaches out to us and hold it. We have to
make our home in that love, to become thoroughly convinced
of it, to live it out in every moment and every dimension of our
life. We have to let it become our very breath.

Some may object: Does not the awareness that God loves
us no matter what, lead to quietism and spiritual laziness? Rea-
sonable as this apprehension may be in theory, in reality the opposite is true. The more rooted we are in love the more generously shall we live our faith and put it into practice. According
to St. Bernard we reach the highest degree of pure love when we
finally love ourselves in God and because of God. Then love has
become freedom. It has released us from intricacies and incon-
sistencies and has led us to a single-heartedness for which the
beatitudes promise the vision of God.

The knowledge that God loves us enables us to love ourselves without excuse and without questioning. We love our-

selves as we are because faith has convinced us that God does so. We are perfectly happy because we no longer worry about our own perfection or our own happiness. All that counts is his love, his will, *he*. Such a faith is tantamount to the perfect fulfillment of the law. It will observe the smallest details of every obligation, not in order to earn or safeguard God's love, but as an outcome of an inner certainty and peace; not in a spirit of pharisaic hair-splitting, but with the freedom of a child of God; not as in a constricting straightjacket, but as a source of pure and deep joy. In living our being-loved we are beyond both the oppressive demands which we impose on ourselves and the noncommittal fickleness of not making choices. Indeed, the faith in God's love liberates us from all inner pressure and at the same time leads us to a complete commitment. "Do not think", Jesus said in the Sermon on the Mount, "that I have come to abolish the law and the prophets. I have come, not to abolish them, but to fulfill them" (Mt 5:17).

It is this love, rather this being-loved, that renders us perfectly docile and obedient to the least sign of God's will. It enables us to transcend our ego ideal, the more or less clear picture of what we would like to be. In this idealistic picture we make up for many real disappointments in our past self-experience. Much frustration may go into this image. It is only partially conscious; its subconscious part especially can exercise an enormous influence in our lives, alas, not always for the good. The prohibitions received since earliest childhood, the accusations and condemnations ever brought against us, the punishments ever inflicted on us, the failures we experienced, all are ingrained in our mind and gradually form a pattern that greatly restricts our freedom.

This mold, without our realizing it, can act as a tyrannical interior master. It gives rise to inhibitions and rationalizations. It can be very rigid and unyielding and also tends to be quite unrealistic. Yet, if we trespass its strict regulations, the ego ideal punishes us with tense feelings of remorse, shame and inferiority. It suppresses the vital forces in us and often renders them suspect: e. g., it can crudely misrepresent tenderness as sensuality, resoluteness as self-complacency, taste for beauty as indulgence in luxury, self-confidence as a lack of humility. These in-

vigorating, positive qualities are necessary for human fulfillment and indispensable for the spreading of the Kingdom. They
should not be suppressed but released; in fact, this is precisely
what happens when we grow in the realization of being loved by
God. Not quietism, but personal and communal unfolding will
be the fruit of this faith.

The Father is glorified in our bearing much fruit. This blos-
soming of our personality is threatened from without and from
within. Usually the latter danger is the greater. If the conscious
or subconscious ego ideal dominates our life, harmony and
peace are hampered. Unable to be true to self, we will be prone
to extremes toward which we are almost compulsively driven.
These unhealthy tendencies can very well be clothed in terms of
religion and piety. Some examples are: excessive orderliness or
thriftiness (easily mixed up with obedience or evangelical poverty), fastidious ritualism, an ultra left or an ultra right stance, an
extremely conservative or an extremely liberal attitude, an ex-
cessively supernatural or an extravagantly secularized approach
to life.

These and similar signals indicate that a person's true self is
stifled and that real fruitfulness is blocked. Authentic faith un-
fetters the heart. True faith gives way to the vitality and fertility
which God has put into man and woman and establishes the
harmony meant for us. What St. Paul describes as the fruit of
the Spirit is as good a description of this harmony as one could
wish: "Love, joy, peace, patient endurance, kindness, generosity, faith, mildness, and chastity" (Gal 5:22-23). A Flemish poet
expresses this ideal in a more exuberant way: "I want to love you
in such a way that I lose all consciousness of my love and grow
in the consciousness of yours. To love you means to forget that I
love while I am overwhelmed by the One who loves. To love you
is to become aware of you and to die to self-awareness. Does
not all self-knowledge degenerate into self-adoration if it is not
flowing steadily into you like a river into the sea? It is your di-
vinity only that gives rhythm to my humanity."[3]

This type of faith is never the result of reasoning or argu-
ing. It is a fruit that normally matures in prayer where the realization of God's acceptance is deepened. There are plenty of
texts in Scripture which can help us for such meditations. Some

collected from the Old Testament are:

> The most High shielded his people and cared for them,
>> guarding them as the apple of his eye.
> As an eagle incites its nestlings forth
>> by hovering over its brood,
> So he spreads his wings to receive them
>> and bore them up on his pinions (Dt 32:10-11).

> He rides the heavens to your rescue,...
> The God of old, he is your refuge.
> Here below, he is the age-old arm
>> driving the enemy before you (Dt 33:26-27 JB).

> But now, thus says the Lord,...
> Fear not, for I have redeemed you;
>> I have called you by name: you are mine.
> When you pass through the water, I will be with you;
>> in the rivers you shall not drown.
> When you walk through fire, you shall not be burned;
>> the flames shall not consume you....
> Because you are precious in my eyes and glorious,
>> and because I love you.
> I give men in return for you
>> and peoples in exchange for your life.
> Fear not, for I am with you (Is 43:1, 2, 4, 5).

> Hear me, O house of Jacob,
>> all who remain of the house of Israel,
> My burden since your birth,
>> whom I have carried from your infancy.
> Even to your old age I am the same,
>> even when your hair is gray I will bear you;
> It is I who have done this, I who will continue,
>> and I who will carry you to safety (Is 46:3-4).

> See, upon the palms of my hands
>> I have written your name (Is 49:16).

Though the mountains leave their place
    and the hills be shaken,
My love shall never leave you,
    nor my covenant of peace be shaken,
    says the Lord,
    who has mercy on you (Is 54:10)

I have loved you with an everlasting love,
    so I am constant in my affection for you (Jer
    31: 3 JB).

The Lord, your God, is in your midst,
    a mighty savior;
He will rejoice over you with gladness,
    and renew you in his love,
He will sing joyfully because of you,
    as one sings at festivals (Zep 3:17-18).

Your love is better than life itself,...(Ps 63:3 JB).

Merciful and gracious is the Lord,
    slow to anger and abounding in kindness (Ps
    103:8, cf Ex 34:6-7).

In the New Testament God's love becomes flesh and blood
in the person of Jesus. In him it receives hands and feet, a face
and a voice so that we can see and hear it. The sole purpose of
the incarnation is to convince us of this faithful love: "The
reason I was born, the reason why I came into the world, is to
testify to the truth" (i. e., reliability of God's love; Jn 18:37).
The love between Father and Son is communicated to us. This
love is the origin of all love and all life. It is the most powerful
and radical (i. e., grasped at the roots) reality. It is shared with
us! Nothing less!! The Father loves us with the same love with
which he loves his Son; he loves his Son in us and us in his Son.
He loves us into images of his Son and his Son into the firstborn
of us all. The Son loves us with the same love with which he
loves his Father; he loves the Father in us and us in the Father.
He loves us as children of his Father whom he so intensely loves,

and he loves his Father as the creator of each of us. In loving us that much, the Son glorifies his Father in us, and the Father glorifies the Son in us. We are taken up into the most intimate and the most fecund of all mysteries: the love between Father and Son in the Holy Spirit. What greater happiness can we experience than that which flows into us from the very Source of all happiness, love and life? The incarnation introduces us into that mystery.

John gives us the key to the life of Jesus in his prologue and again at the very beginning of the passion: "He empowered them to become children of God.... We have seen his glory: the glory of an only Son coming from the Father, filled with an enduring love" (1:12, 14). "He had loved his own in this world, and would show his love for them to the end" (Jn 13:1). Every incident in Jesus' life could be cited here as an affirmation of this mission. Let us only remark that God's love in Jesus has two hands, so to speak: the one hand is forgiveness which holds us even in our guilt, the other hand being the resurrection which reveals to us that God holds us even beyond death. Indeed, "neither death nor life...neither height nor depth nor any other creature, will be able to separate us from the love of God that comes to us in Christ Jesus, our Lord" (Rm 8:38-39). The recapitulation of Jesus' life inspires St. Paul to a prayer:

> That is why I kneel before the Father from whom every family in heaven and on earth takes its name; and I pray that he will bestow on you gifts in keeping with the riches of his glory. May he strengthen you inwardly through the working of his Spirit. May Christ dwell in your hearts through faith, and may charity be the root and foundation of your life. Thus you will be able to grasp fully, with all the holy ones, the breadth and length and height and depth of Christ's love, and experience this love which surpasses all knowledge, so that you may attain to the fullness of God himself (Eph 3:14-19).

> We thank you, God, that you watch over us, that it is not blind fate which shapes our lives.

Your concern is for each of us.
You go with us on all our ways.
You remain faithful to us,
more than a father is attached to his firstborn,
more than a mother who cannot forget the child of
her womb.
You know our names
and you set the deepest in us free.
In Jesus your faithful concern became visible.
He is the man who lived for others.
We believe that he is still alive and with us,
your Son and our Lord,
today and every day, for ever and ever. Amen.

SIX

THE JOY OF THE FATHER

Among all the images of God that exist there is only one that does him full justice, the man Jesus of Nazareth. St. Paul never tires of singing the paean of the surpassing knowledge of his Lord Jesus Christ in whom he has found 'his wealth', the God he sought so over-zealously in the days when he was a Pharisee. "In Christ the fullness of deity resides in bodily form....He is the image (Greek: *eikon;* hence icon) of the invisible God....It pleased God to make absolute fullness reside in him..." (Col 2:9; 1:15, 19). In him we "may attain to the fullness of God himself" (Eph 3:19). In him "the kindness and love of God our Savior appeared" (Ti 3:4), and nothing "can ever come between us and the love of God made visible in Christ Jesus our Lord" (Rm 8:39 JB). In Jesus God's love became visible and tangible. Johannine christology is no less explicit: "No one has ever seen God. It is God the only Son, ever at the Father's side, who has revealed him" (Jn 1:18). "Whoever has seen me has seen the Father" (Jn 14:9). "Whoever looks on me is seeing him who sent me" (Jn 12:45). "The Father and I are one...The Father is in me and I in him" (Jn 10:30, 38). Jesus is the beloved Son, the glory and joy of his Father.

All the other New Testament authors join Paul and John in giving to Jesus "the name that is above every other name, so that at Jesus' name every knee must bend in the heavens, on the earth, and under the earth" (Phil 2:10). In fact, the whole content of their writings is not so much doctrine or message as the person of Jesus Christ. He himself is *the* Word spoken, the ultimate self-manifestation of God The epitome of the Good News is not that Jesus is God, but rather that God is as he appears in Jesus. The New Testament shows the uniqueness of Jesus from many angles with indefatigable enthusiasm.

This chapter will limit itself to one particular aspect of Jesus' uniqueness. A good transition into this specific topic seems the statement that among the many revolutionaries of human history, Jesus of Nazareth takes first place. In fact, he is so much a revolutionist that he transcends the category and consequently, it would be misleading and unfair to ascribe simply this epithet to him. He wants us to reform ourselves first and not to start by reforming other people - this makes him already a little odd among most revolutionaries. But the decisive uniqueness of Jesus as a revolutionist lies in the object of his reform; it was one which nobody before or after him ever had the courage to deal with so thoroughly, namely, guilt. He undertakes the remarkable feat of transforming the bitter suffering of guilt into an experience of deep joy.

It may not be obvious that guilt is such a common and bitter pain. Only a person who has had access to the inner chambers of many human hearts will realize the agony in this suffering. It is usually the last secret a person gives away. It is kept hidden, if not repressed, at almost any cost. Yet behind the facade it is there, exercising its painful and devastating influence. The more it is repressed, the more it infects and spoils everything else, most of all every genuine joy. I don't feel at home anymore in my own skin. I feel like a hypocrite, a fraud. If people only knew who I really am, they would all reject me. I do not really belong to them. This feeling haunts me even in the midst of a celebration or in the company of a good friend; yes, most of all in that company! I feel like a split person, alienated from my true self. I do not understand myself. I just cannot comprehend how I could do a thing like this or keep on doing it. There is a dichotomy in my very being. Paul gives the classic description of this predicament: "I cannot even understand my own actions. I do not do what I want to do but what I hate... What happens is that I do, not the good I will to do, but the evil I do not intend" (Rm 7:15, 19).

This heartache is aggravated by the fact that there is no way to get rid of guilt. It haunts. One may try to escape into compensations and repression, but it continues haunting nevertheless. I have met people who had made generous, almost heroic sacrifices to free themselves from guilt feelings; it just did not work. A psychiatrist can help a person to become conscious of it, to relive the experience, to verbalize it, to objectify it; but if it is real guilt, he cannot take it away. To be sure, there are inauthentic guilt feelings which need to be cured and where psychiatric help can be appropriate and indispensable. The remedy for real guilt however is beyond the realm of human professionalism.

The evil we commit has something mysterious about it. We cannot really grasp it. It is so alluring, easy, obvious, yet it is so senseless and frustrating. It shuns the light and proliferates in the dark. "Everyone who practices evil hates the light; he does not come near it for fear his deeds will be exposed" (Jn 3:20). We have difficulty getting a clear look at it. It is always a combination of weakness and malice intermingled in an inseparable way. There is most certainly always a fair amount of weakness in our sins. No one sits down to think: 'Well, can't I dream up some evil to commit?' That would be sheer caricature. We do not conjure up evil; it jumps right at us. We fight it. We don't want to do it. We resist it vehemently, but eventually we yield... sometimes. Yes, there is much frailty in us; it would be unfair not to mention this. Yet there is also the other element. It is not only powerlessness. It is a matter of unwillingness as well. There is something in me that wants the evil and takes sides with the weakness and opts for it. There is something in me that wills the frailty, and in some cases even fosters it. The interplay of the two - the inability and the malice - is very subtle. There is no dividing line, be it ever so thin, between the one and the other; that line simply does not exist. Like warp and woof weave the fabric, like two liquids that mix perfectly, maliciousness and weakness blend together to create the evil. The degree of guilt distinct from frailty can never be measured precisely.

Since evil is a mysterious reality, we cannot fully articulate it. It is like an iceberg, nine-tenths of which remains under water; no one could ever lift all or even most of it above the water to make it visible. This accounts for the common feeling of not having really said it all when confessing my sins. This impression is very accurate. If I would try to express in words all my sins and sinfulness, I try the impossible and wind up in a blind alley. What is even more important, however, is that I would tend to put the emphasis in the wrong place. Perhaps I even try to turn confession into a bookkeeping feat or an achievement of self-justification instead of a reception of God's liberal and liberating grace. This is not to say that the verbalization of our sinfulness can be neglected, but that its effectiveness is inevitably limited. In a certain sense one could say that the words we speak in confessing our sins have a token value - they stand for much more sinfulness than we can possibly tell. All this adds up to saying that it is impossible for us to handle authentic guilt. It is not only an excruciating, all-penetrating pain, but also there is no way out for us.

If we expand this topic so as to include collective guilt, the problem becomes even more burdensome and unwieldy. We have recently begun to be more aware of the evil which we evoke or continue together as a group, a nation, a culture. No one in particular can be held responsible, yet this evil persists only because all of us in our communal lifestyle sustain it. We begin to see that our personal guilt is linked through countless fibres with the guilt of all of us. After thirty centuries we experience in a wider scope what the psalmist expressed: "Indeed, in guilt was I born, and in sin my mother conceived me" (51:7). We do not take this as an excuse, but as an illustration of the extent to which we are entangled in evil. We feel even more unable to cope with collective guilt than with individual guilt and are tempted all the more strongly to play the ostrich.

The greatness of Jesus becomes manifest in his tackling this elusive problem, this age-old suffering. His name, in Jewish thinking more markedly than in ours, signifies his mission and his identity: "You are to name him Jesus because he will save his people from their sins" (Mt 1:21). He came to liberate and to forgive, to recreate and to trigger the good. The crushing reality of guilt he turns into a launching pad for a most freeing and joyful happening. In Russia a person who has failed is exiled to a hard-labor camp in Siberia or assigned to a psychiatric institution. In the gospel such a person is treated to a celebration in which he gets the honor seat and meets with an intense happiness. This is the great revolution Jesus of Nazareth stands for. The depth of our negative feelings is changed into the height of an equally positive experience. The burden is taken from our shoulders. We can dance with relief and delight. As St. Augustine said to the people of Hippo: "put your sins under your feet and they will raise you up to heaven."

To be truly receptive to this surprise and to really celebrate the feast we need to take off our masks and lay down our arms. As long as we think we can manage by ourselves, we are not yet ready for the turn-around. The ideal which the gospel sets before us is extremely high. It seems that there are only two ways to deal with it. We can cut corners so as to reduce it to a manageable size, i. e., make an anthology of our favorite passages and leave it at that. The other way is to take the gospel as it is and attempt to live it to the full. But then we shall soon find out that we fail many times each day. If we learn how to live on God's forgiveness, our failure will not prevent us from being the thoroughly happy people the gospel wants us to be. If we do not find the way to the divine pardon, the evangelical challenge will become an oppressive burden that renders us gloomy and despondent. The gospel then becomes bad news instead of good.

The pluriformity which came into the Church in the wake of Vatican II is surely beneficial. Uniformity stifles life and creates only a semblance of unity, whereas true union differentiates. That is not to say that it is always easy to live the oneness in the pluriformity, but at least we have the certainty that this challenge is in line with "the way, the truth and the life" of Jesus. Yet no one will be surprised to find out that pluriformity involves some risks as well. One of these is that it can offer an escape to avoid metanoia which is so essential in Jesus' proclamation of the Kingdom - that deep change in the set of our priorities that makes our lives different. The danger is that we choose from the large variety in the supply of ecclesiastical and spiritual values precisely those elements that confirm our ways. Yet in truth we may not need confirmation, but conversion. In that case the road that leads to the heart of the Good News, to the experience of forgiveness is blocked.

If we want to enter into the core-experience of Jesus' message, we have to unmask, disarm and open up to conversion. Jesus agrees fully with the rhetorical question of the Pharisees, "Who can forgive sins except God alone?" (Mk 2:7). Forgiveness of sins is indeed something exclusively divine. We cannot achieve it; we can only let it happen to us. It means to share in the confession of Good Friday and the absolution of Easter. It is entering deeply into Jesus' mission, allowing him to be, not in a general but in a personal way, savior; the one who saves me from my sins.

Though the emphasis is entirely on the receptive part we play in this wonder, yet we have to let it happen to us and that implies some activity on our part. We have to verbalize our sins and sinfulness. Why? It is not because God wants us to grovel before he is willing to forgive. It is even less an attempt to tell God something which he does not already know. It surely is not meant as a painstaking achievement that earns absolution. It is the human way in which we prepare our hearts to receive the divine gift of forgiveness. It is clearing the road and creating room for what surpasses us. It marks the difference between remorse which is caught up in a self-centered monologue, and contrition which leads to an other-directed dialogue. The problem of forgiveness is not with God; it is with us. It is not easy to absorb and to comprehend this enormous liberation. It is not easy to let forgiveness flow into our bloodstream and to have all the poison of guilt washed away. To express in words our guilt is part of this process and therefore part of the sacrament itself.

Yet we may still feel a difficulty. If I have offended someone, I may find it dishonest to (ab)use a secret confession as a substitute for a courageous and frank reconciliation with that particular person. And rightly so! Authentic regret imples that I in one way or another apologize to this person. But then, why not leave it at the apology and perhaps even restitution, and omit confession? It is true, of course, that in offending that person I at the same time also offended God who is Father of that person, or if one prefers, the deepest Ground of his or her being. but then, with equal right, is not the reconcilation with that person at the same time a reconciliation with God, and confession superfluous? Well, not really! In offending, one act may affect both creature and Creator; in reconciliation this is not so; there, two distinct reparations are necessary. Some examples in human relations that support this fact are not hard to imagine.

No matter how secondary and no matter how painful personal confession is, I cannot get around it in case of serious guilt. Yet though it is necessary, it is by no means the heart of the matter - forgiveness is! St. Augustine describes the liberating experience of having the load of guilt taken away as a waking-up to God's merciful love. It is like an oppressive dream in which I feel utterly rejected and which is suddenly dispelled when I awake to a bright new day. The difference however is that guilt is not a dream but a powerful reality. So the thrill of coming to a new day in the merciful love of God is all the greater. "In the tender compassion of our God the dawn from on high shall break upon us" (Lk 1:78). His mercy is as gentle and as certain as the dawn. It is the experience of the prodigal son who felt hardly worthy to be accepted as a hired hand, yet found himself cordially embraced and the center of a wonderful celebration. The reaction of his father surpassed his wildest expectations. The joy of the father was so pure and so great that he brought his son back to life. The grief of the father was all for the son; none was for himself. His anguish was completely unselfish. St. Thomas Aquinas explains: "God is not offended by us except in so far as we act against our own proper good".[1] This remark is one more way to confirm that God is love. Even in his being offended, he is nothing but love.

The revolution which Jesus brings consists in the fact that it is precisely *in* the forgiveness that the younger son learns to know his father. Both the younger and the elder son have always known that their father was a good man; but *how* good he was, only the sinner finds out! Forgiveness makes the last one first, and the first last. Before the brother's coming home, the elder son was closer to his father, literally and figuratively, whereas the younger one was far away in a distant country, estranged from his father. At the moment of forgiveness the roles are changed. From now onwards it is the younger son who has entered into a new intimacy with his father. While he senses how pure and deep the joy of his father is, he begins to understand the selfless sincerity of the man's love. This in turn creates a new closeness with the father to which the elder brother is only an outsider. Indeed this is revolution. Loss is turned into gain. The depth of misery is changed into a peak of joy. The most devastating experience is transformed into an extremely fruitful event. The restless desperation of guilt becomes an unspeakably intimate experience of God.

In the blissful experience of his father's forgiveness the younger son comes not only to a new insight into his father's goodness but also into his own sin. One would expect the sequence to be: consciousness of sin, contrition, asking for forgiveness. A closer look however shows a reversed order. It is only the forgiveness that really reveals the sin. As stressed above we cannot grasp evil; consequently, the right reaction to sin and sinfulness is a grace. True contrition is a gift rather than an achievement. It is not so much the result of introspection as of contemplating the Lord's love. It is more a fruit of prayer than of examining oneself. The acme of contrition is reached in the self-forgetting move of entering into God's forgiveness.

Authentic contrition is not morose; there is a genuine peace in it. It is worked in us by the Spirit and is characterized by the fruits of the Spirit, among which are love, joy, peace, mildness and kindness. As a comparison we can think of a good friend who points out a mistake we made; he may be perfectly blunt, yet there is an atmosphere of affirmative trust and encouragement in his manner of bringing it home to us. An enemy however could sharply criticize us for that mistake and tear us to pieces. Likewise in the spiritual life, the enemy can easily be recognized from the discouragement he infuses. God always inspires hope, peace and courage.

From now onward, the sin is no longer mine. It is taken away from me by the Lamb of God, who took it upon himself and thus carried it out of my life and out of this world. It would then be unfair to hold on to it. A new space has been created in which I can breathe freely. Remission means that a new mission is given to me, a renewed trust. In fact, true mission starts only with remission. Really fruitful service is possible only as a result of experiencing forgiveness. As long as I have not encountered this kernel of the gospel, my service tends to be self-centered. The spirit of the Sermon on the Mount comes to life only in the climate of repentance and forgiveness. This is where the gospel really begins; all else so far has been only introduction. Jesus' first word in Mark's Gospel is: "The time has come and the kingdom of God is close at hand. Repent, and believe the Good News" (Mk 1:15 JB). In this spirit - the Holy Spirit - we can love as we know ourselves loved by God and serve as Jesus served us. "O happy fault!"

> Merciful Father,
> let us not seek false names for our sins
> nor let us deny the evil we commit.
> May the gentle light of your truth
> lead us into the wonder of your forgiveness
> and there open us to a new depth of your love.
> Let us know the joy with which you receive and embrace us
> whenever we return to you.
> Make us share in that joy
> and so become new persons
> venturing a new beginning in our service,
> ready to pass on your reconciliation and your peace to all,
> today and every day, for ever and ever. Amen.

SEVEN

FISHING MEN

Several psalms express gratitude for God's forgiveness and at the same time the desire to announce his goodness to others. Thus David in Psalm 51 prays:

> I will teach transgressors your ways,
>   and sinners shall return to you.
> Free me from blood guilt, O God, my saving God;
>   then my tongue shall revel in your justice.
> O Lord, open my lips,
>   and my mouth shall proclaim your praise
>   (v 15-17).

As the prodigal son discovered a new dimension in his father's love and entered into a much deeper intimacy with him, so we discern a new significance in the person of Jesus which we simply have to share with others. He is no longer merely a demanding standard of conduct, a high ideal we want to live up to, but he has become the one to whom we owe our life, our personal wholeness. This prompts us to become apostles.

The change of a 'sinful man' into an apostle 'catching men' is explicit in Simon Peter (Lk 5:1-11). The miraculous haul of fish has obvious apostolic overtones and is clearly directed toward the climactic end. While the professional fisherman is reschooled to be a fisher of men, some basic characteristics of the apostolate are illustrated. As we contemplate the scene, let us be open for a change of heart that will make our lives more apostolic. We pray that in this meditation we may come to know the Lord more clearly, to love him more dearly, to follow him more nearly, and to proclaim him more sincerely.

The passage has three parts. In each of them the initiative is taken by Jesus.

Listening to the Word

As Jesus stood by Lake Gennesaret, and the crowd pressed in on him to hear the word of God, he saw two boats moored by the side of the lake; the fishermen had disembarked and were washing their nets. He got into one of the boats, the one belonging to Simon, and asked him to pull out a short distance from the shore; then, remaining seated, he continued to teach the crowds from the boat.

Jesus is speaking to the people, not in the synagogue as formerly, but to the crowd in the open. He uses Simon's boat - an external service of Peter in this preliminary stage of his ministry. For the time being Peter's main task is to listen to the Master along with the rest of the people. The foundation of all apostolate is "faith in what you heard" (as Paul says twice in Gal 3:2, 5), and that necessarily begins with listening. Listening means to open up to something that comes from the outside. Initially it may sound strange and disturb our mindset; eventually it may have far-reaching consequences.

True listening therefore requires humble courage. Jesus warns: "Take heed how you hear" (Lk 8:18). One can listen in many ways! Our listening can degenerate into a filtering process that lets through only what suits us and rejects from the outside whatever does not confirm our stance. Genuine listening implies that we not only empty ourselves to a certain degree, but also more specifically, that we make ourselves receptive. We could be tempted to listen like a master, not in order to learn, but only to check on others. One of the outstanding gifts of the Servant of Yahweh is mentioned in his third song: "Each morning the

Lord Yahweh wakes me to hear, to listen like a disciple. The
Lord Yahweh has opened my ear" (Is 50:4-5 JB). We ask for a
disciple's ear to listen to Jesus speaking now from Peter's boat
and often in manifold other ways.

The word of God is more than an articulation of a thought
or feeling. It is alive. The Hebrew word *bara* used for Yahweh
means both to speak and to create. God speaks creatures. His
word is spirit, that is, life-giving, as is suggested for instance in
the parallelism of this psalm verse: "By the word of the Lord the
heavens were made; by the breath of his mouth all their host"
(Ps 33:6). It is effective:

> For just as from the heavens
>   the rain and snow come down
> And do not return there
>   till they have watered the earth,
>   making it fertile and fruitful,
> Giving seed to him who sows
>   and bread to him who eats,
> So shall my word be
>   that goes forth from my mouth;
> It shall not return to me void,
>   but shall do my will,
>   achieving the end for which I sent it (Is 55:10-11).

The word of God is powerful like fire, like a hammer shattering rocks (Jer 23:29). Above all it is living - it has a history. It
was addressed to Abraham making him leave his country. It
sent Moses to liberate his people. There is also a low-tide in the
history of the word of God: "It was rare for Yahweh to speak in
those days" (1 Sm 3:1 JB), so rare, in fact, that even the highpriest Eli did not recognize it until the third time. The word of
God is entrusted to the prophets to pass on to the people; it
speaks through them. It takes hold of them like a fire burning in
their heart, searing in their bones (Jer 20:9). It fills them with a
divine power.

> See, I place my words in your mouth!
>   This day I set you

> over nations and over kingdoms,
> To root up and to tear down,
> to destroy and to demolish,
> to build and to plant (Jer 1:9-10).

Then comes the zenith in the history of God's word: "In times past, God spoke in fragmentary and varied ways to our fathers through the prophets; in this, the final age, he has spoken to us through his son" (Heb 1:1-2). "When the designated time had come, God sent forth his son born of a woman" (Gal 4:4) and "The Word became flesh" (Jn 1:14). The Word of God now walks the earth in person:

> The heavens were opened, and as I looked on, a white horse appeared; its rider was called 'The Faithful and True.' Justice is his standard in passing judgment and in waging war. His eyes blazed like fire, and on his head were many diadems. Inscribed on his person was a name known to no one but himself. He wore a cloak that had been dipped in blood, and his name was the Word of God (Rv 19:11-13).

The word of God has power to touch hearts and to heal: "The people were spellbound by Jesus' teaching, for his words had authority" (Lk 4:32). "Power went out from him which cured all" (Lk 6:19).

The history of the word of God is continued in the Church. It is her task to keep God's word alive and to transmit it in a living, appealing way. At the time of his ascension Jesus tells his disciples: "Go into the whole world and proclaim the good news to all creation" (Mk 16:15). The whole Church has to preach the whole gospel to the whole world. Everybody in the Church has an apostolic responsibility which cannot be shunted to a few 'professionals'. The gospel must be preached undiluted, intact and above all alive. The whole world, entitled as it is to hear the good news, is to be evangelized.

This ministry of the word is closely connected with prayer and even mentioned in one breath with prayer by the Twelve (Acts 6:4). In prayer the word of God can take deep roots provided there is a willingness to act honestly upon it. Meditation on the words of Scripture will eventualy evolve into contemplation of the Word Incarnate. The many words zero in on the one Word. Listening becomes gazing at Jesus, reasoning develops into looking at the Lord. The center shifts from the head to the heart. "Meditation is the mother of love, contemplation her daughter" (St. Francis de Sales).

*****

The miraculous catch of fish

When Jesus had finished speaking he said to Simon, "Put out into deep water and lower your nets for a catch." Simon answered, "Master, we have been hard at it all night long and have caught nothing; but if you say so, I will lower the nets." Upon doing this they caught such a great number of fish that their nets were at the breaking point. They signaled to their mates in the other boat to come and help them. These came, and together they filled the two boats until they nearly sank.

It has been a long night of hard labor - all in vain. They netted only a load of frustrated fatigue. Now the Lord tells them to lower the nets once more. "You are a carpenter; we are fishermen. We know the lake; it is our domain. It is dead now, closed, no catch, no promise. If it does not yield anything during the night, then certainly not in daytime." But the Lord sends them back. He does not give in to their down-heartedness. He considers their resignation out of place. He is used to the improbable. After all he is 'the master of the impossible' (Charles de Foucauld). They may be experts, but they still have to learn the power of the word of God.

Indeed, it is their lake, their domain; so he sends them back into it - into the unpromising void. The skeptical, weary persons of our age are committed to us: people plagued by inflation and worried about recession and unemployment; dulled by the media and doped by the consumer society; people who scorn spirituality and just want facts, accomplishments and money;

who are scared of projection and for whom God is very vague; people whose work is their prayer and their idol - this kind of people we have to bait for God. When we set out for deep water, we better not harbor any illusions. It is mission impossible. We have no chance. It is a waste of time and efforts, and ridiculous at that. Today's apostles do not come as successful, venerable characters but rather as poor, somewhat lonely people. They are certain of this one thing: that it is not easy to win hearts for the living God - and also, thank heaven, that they can build on the word of this living God. In the last analysis they have no other guarantee.

The word of God is powerful, indeed, but it has to be put into practice if it is ever to display its power. "Upon doing this" they make their catch! In the storms of the apostolic life we can hold our ground if we live the word.

> Why do you call me 'Lord, Lord,' and not put into practice what I teach you? Any man who desires to come to me will hear my words and put them into practice. I will show you with whom he is to be compared. He may be likened to the man who, in building a house, dug deeply and laid the foundtion on a rock. When the floods came the torrent rushed in on that house, but failed to shake it because of its solid foundation. On the other hand, anyone who has heard my words but not put them into practice is like the man who built his house on the ground without any foundation. When the torrent rushed upon it, it immediately fell in and was completely destroyed (Lk 6:46-49).

The time will come when the word of God is the only support that can give meaning to our mission.

In the strength of this word, the apostles find life where all looked dead, a catch where appeared only emptiness, openness where everything seemed closed. An unassuming and simple attitude will loosen hearts that until now remained tight. We will find out to our happy surprise that in the faceless despondency of many there is much more longing for God than we ever imagined if only we reach them on the right wavelength. Why do tens of thousands of young people from all over Europe and even from across the Atlantic make their way every summer to the remote village of Taizé in France to spend days or weeks (and sometimes years) in primitive lodging with the ecumenical community of the Brothers? Why are hundreds of Roman adolescents praying together daily in San Egidio, pooling their spare money and serving the poor of the run-down Trastevere neighborhood, all the while radiating an unabashed joy and enthusiasm? Why do twenty plus girls enter Mother Teresa's Missionaries of Charity every month, heading for an extremely poor life of nothing but prayer and service to the destitute? Why are basic Christian communities in Latin America growing like grass despite cruel attempts to intimidate them? Why is prayer such a hunger that people are eagerly looking for gurus, if need be, in India or Japan?

The straightforward trust in the Lord's word is rewarded by a staggering haul of fish. Some years later, Peter in another shocking setting is given another message of risk. During noon prayer he is invited to the repugnant act of eating impure food. "Sir", comes his instant reaction, "it is unthinkable! I have never eaten anything unclean or impure in my life" (Acts 10:14). It soon becomes clear however that this is really a call to put out into the deep water of the pagan world and to take the lead in accepting Gentiles into the Christian community. "What God has purified you are not to call unclean" (Acts 10:15; 11:9) turns out to have a broader application than to food only - it applies most of all to people! Peter learned an important lesson: "God has made it clear to me that no one should call any man unclean or impure" (Acts 10:28). Actually, this triggers a most surprising catch since it marks the initiation of the rapid, worldwide expansion of the early Church.

Today we are called to risk and trust once more. Stripped of our pretensions, we have to venture into the deep water of our secularized world. The best way to keep the faith is to spread it, not restricting ourselves to the areas where we feel safe, but reaching out. Courageous faith in the power of God's word coupled with an open-minded humility prepares us to discover God where his name is never mentioned. If we leave the

stronghold of our self assumed superiority, we shall meet smoldering coals of faith which we thus far had tended to overlook,
misread or quench. Indicative of faith, though implicit, may be
actions to protect life and to promote the quality of life; an opposition, perhaps a bit clumsy, to the affluent establishment; a
lonely attempt to keep one's integrity in a society of overt and
hidden persuaders; a liberal effort for justice on a small or
worldwide scale; actual, personal service to under-privileged
countries; private, grassroot help in one's neighborhood; a patient search for interiority, and many more phenomena.

None of these may be impeccable; yet all of them deserve
our respect and cooperation. To apply untimely standards of
perfectionism could well be a lack of faith, trust and love.
Faultfinding is an ineffective way to build the Kingdom of God.
In the harsh times of the Reformation the sensitive bishop of
Geneva acted on the principle that one catches more flies with a
spoonful of honey than with a barrel of vinegar. The farmer
who sowed the good seed also forbade his men to pull up the
weeds lest the wheat would be taken along with them (Mt
13:24-30, 36-43), and the Servant of Yahweh is cited for not
breaking the bruised reed (Is 42:3). The safest way toward apostolic fruitfulness is to take the risk of really loving.

*****

Adoration and mission

At the sight of this, Simon Peter fell at the knees of
Jesus saying, "Leave me, Lord. I am a sinful man."
For indeed, amazement at the catch they had made
seized him and all his shipmates, as well as James
and John, Zebedee's sons, who were partners with
Simon. Jesus said to Simon, "Do not be afraid.
From now on you will be catching men." With that
they brought their boats to land, left everything,
and became his followers.

In the miracle Peter has recognized Jesus as Lord. By now many
people had come upon Jesus. They were intrigued, won-
dered for a while, hesitated, thought 'yes', figured 'no', and

most of them went on. Few really encountered him. Little people are dealt with easily enough, but it is scary to encounter a truly great person. For Peter this was the closest contact with Jesus he had yet experienced. Overcome with awe, his instant reaction was to draw back. Like the prophet Isaiah, Peter realized in the presence of the holy one the unbearable contrast: "Woe is me, I am doomed! For I am a man of unclean lips, living among a people of unclean lips; yet my eyes have seen the King, the Lord of hosts!" (Is 6:5). Both the prophet and the apostle make a statement about their sinfulness, but even more about the Lord's holiness.

The shock and awe come at the end of this episode; yet they are really the beginning of a new life: "With that they brought their boats to land, left everything, and became his followers". The miracle illustrates what vocation and mission are; rather vocation and mission are the actual miracle. Vocation means an invitation to something which is beyond us. It implies an awe which does not render us blind, but makes us discern God's strength in our weakness so that we dare our mission. It means a reverence from which unwholesome fear is filtered out while a consciousness of the divine presence remains with us throughout our mission.

This happened to Abraham and Moses, to Elijah and Isaiah, and to all the other men and women of God. In fact there is no divine mission which does not begin with such an awesome encounter. It is this immersion into 'the totally other One', this close contact with the mystery of the all-holy God that makes us new persons. Saul will have a similar experience on the road to Damascus and after him many more people. It happens in a sudden, overwhelming moment or in a prolonged desert period. Sometimes it is carefully longed for, but it may also take people totally by surprise. For many persons a serious retreat has been the setting.

This deep inner experience however cannot remain hidden in their heart of hearts. It affects their behavior and lifestyle and renders them convincing witnesses to what they have sensed of God. If we call it a consecration, it is not so much consecration *for* a mission as a consecration which *is* a mission. Adoration and apostolate are not opposites; they go together; in fact, they presuppose each other. Karl Rahner was bold enough to state quite bluntly: "The devout Christian of the future will either be a 'mystic', one who has 'experienced' something, or he will cease to be anything at all."[1]

The younger generation especially looks to the apostle for what is beyond his or her professional competence; only this 'beyond' makes the ministry authentic. An Indian bishop, who had previously been a college teacher, explained that in the eyes of his students he had been a competent teacher and a trusted counselor, but too little a witness to God. Out of a student body of a thousand, sixty were Catholics. They appreciated their professor and came to see him about their practical, ethical and scholastic problems, but thirteen of his best Catholic students used to go to a pious Hindu 'to sit with God'. He concluded: "I was not referring sufficiently to God." Yet that is the quintessence of apostolate.

"Do not be afraid." The word of God that creates and disconcerts also recreates and encourages. Our courage however now has a new foundation - the bottomless majesty and reliability of God. We acknowledge our dependence and find security in it. We surrender ourselves and let the power of God work through us. We commit ourselves wholeheartedly and energetically, but on the spur of God. Such a task we do not assign ourselves. It is not a profession we choose on our own - we are called and sent to it. The apostles left everything for it. 'Everything' may not have been much in their case. Yet 'everything' is all one is able to give and that is always a big thing. Leaving everything to follow the Lord is still the decisive step in a vocation to the apostolate or to the contemplative life. At one time I honestly said Yes to it. What has become of this Yes?

In the appendix of John's Gospel we find a parallel story. One can easily find a dozen relevant details shared by both accounts. The main difference is, of course, that this time the miracle and the missioning take place after the resurrection. It is as though the beginning of Peter's vocation is reiterated, but in the context of some new experiences. Paramount among these is the death and resurrection of the Lord. For Peter personally his betrayal of Jesus also had made a great impact. It left a wound, perhaps more so in Peter than in Jesus. His return to the source of his vocation, the miraculous catch of fish, is meant as a healing and a strengthening - a re-mission. It is by no means an identical replaying of the old tape, but it is a deepening of the experience in new circumstances and an integration of some important new elements into it. Disappointment in himself has painfully rid him of some naive romanticism present in his first call. The forgiveness by the Lord has deepened his intimacy with Jesus. To relive the original call now is valuable in that it prevents him from turning aside from his early love (Rv 2:4). "Lord, you know everything" (Jn 21:17). You know that I love you. You also know that human respect makes me fickle. It is good to be known by you.

Indeed the Lord knows everything. That is our security, our joy. It is a good foundation for the second call. The Lord who has overcome death can also overcome our human frailty. We can abandon ourselves to him. That is a good basis for apostolic ministry. "Lord, you know that I love you" (Jn 21: 15-16) - that is an attitude in which everything that is good can grow.

> We thank you, Father,
> that you have spoken to us
> the Word of eternal life
> and have given your Son as our brother.
> He speaks your love to us,
> giving it flesh and blood in his own life
> and in ours.
> We who call ourselves Christians
> are sent to continue the life of Christ
> in our lives.
> This is not a time to be shallow or half-hearted,
> for the world needs men and women
> who can honestly speak your name
> and witness to your Son.
> We ask you then, Father,
> protect and renew our vocation
> so that we be faithful to the name we bear
> and be appealing witnesses to your kingdom
> today and every day, for ever and ever. Amen.

EIGHT

LIGHT FROM LIGHT

Bartimaeus, the blind beggar, meets him who is the light of the world, receives his sight from him, then follows him (Mk 10:46-52). In all the synoptic gospels this is the last miracle Jesus works before he enters Jerusalem. Placed between the third and last prophecy of the passion and the fulfillment of that prophecy, the meaning of this miracle is to be understood from the position given it by the evangelists.

The disciples fail to grasp the intent of all three prophecies: each time they react in a frustratingly inept way. After the first prophecy of the passion, "Peter took Jesus aside and began to remonstrate with him. At this he turned around and, eyeing the disciples, reprimanded Peter: 'Get out of my sight, you Satan! You are not judging by God's standards but by man's!'" (Mk 8:32-33). It appears that Peter is not following Jesus, but wants Jesus to follow him. That same tendency to judge by man's standards instead of God's, will trip up Peter several times in his later life, notably in the courtyard of the highpriest during Jesus' trial (Lk 22:54-62) and with the Judaizers in Antioch (Gal 2:11-14). The second prophecy follows in the next chapter of Mark. "'The Son of Man is going to be delivered into the hands of men who will put him to death; three days after his death he will rise.' Though they failed to understand his words, they were afraid to question him" (v 31-32). Rather than pursue the meaning of Jesus' words, the disciples in their insensitivity, began to argue as to who is the greatest. While walking with his disciples one day, Jesus prophecied his passion the third time: "We are on our way to Jerusalem, where the Son of Man will be handed over to the chief priests and the scribes. They will condemn him to death and hand him over to the Gentiles, who will mock him and spit at him, flog him, and finally kill him. But three days later he will rise" (Mk 10:33-34). Again Jesus encounters a similar lack of understanding. Immediately after hearing the words, James and John, sons of Zebedee, in ambitious rivalry approach the Lord for a favor: "See to it that we sit, one at your right and the other at your left, when you come into your glory" (Mk 10:37). Right after Jesus had told them he was going to take the last place, the one on the cross, the sons of Zebedee ask for the first places. Then comes the outsider Bartimaeus who begs for sight from Jesus, receives it and joins him on the road to Jerusalem.

The story of the blind beggar is an old story, unadorned, but rich with the inner experiences of the man who discovered in Jesus the true light (Jn 1:9; 9:5). Bartimaeus focuses on Jesus completely and in a number of ways:
- in his cry for pity: "Jesus, Son of David, have pity on me!";
- in his perseverance despite those who rebuke him: "He shouted all the louder";
- in the gesture of throwing off his cloak;
- in his faith: "Your faith has healed you";
- in experiencing Jesus' healing power;
- in joining Jesus on his way.
The name of Jesus seems to pervade the whole passage; it occurs no less than six times in these seven verses! The gospel narrative thus invites us in the manner of Bartimaeus to focus on Jesus in every way so that we too may experience him as the true light and our source of strength as we follow him to Jerusalem.

Luke especially constructs the public life of Jesus as a journey from Galilee to Jerusalem. In the first place, Jerusalem is the city where Jesus' rejection reaches its climax in his passion and death. "O, Jerusalem, Jerusalem, you slay the prophets and stone those who are sent to you!" (Lk 13:34). But later the Father will turn that same city into the scene of the glorious resurrection. It is for this city that Jesus heads so resolutely. As he leaves Jericho, the disciples and a sizeable crowd go with him. At this time of the year the whole community is on the move because all devout Jews were to celebrate the passover festival in Jerusalem. As usual, the people traveled these last eighteen miles in groups for the sake of security and company. To walk with the rabbi of Nazareth, to listen to his words and perhaps even to experience a sensational happening was so enticing that many pilgrims were in his company.

Along the way at the exit road to Jerusalem there sits a beggar, Bartimaeus, son of Timaeus. To sit at the roadside in this particular spot was especially opportune, for the many pilgrims who passed by had a special obligation to give alms. The beggar was blind. Eye diseases were quite common in those eastern towns and villages: the hygiene was poor, medication and treatment rare, medicare non-existent. Blindness mercilessly turns a person into a beggar and puts him at the margin of society. At the roadside, the blind man is a symbol of all poor citizens who do not see any way out of their predicament.

The Jewish nation was familiar with the Scriptures and understood the healing of the blind as a Messianic sign. Many texts in the Old Testament foretell the Messiah as one who 'will open eyes'; let one example suffice:

> I, the Lord, have called you for the
>   victory of justice,
>   I have grasped you by the hand;
> I formed you, and set you
>   as a covenant of the people,
>   a light for the nations,
> To open the eyes of the blind,
>   to bring out prisoners from confinement,
>   and from the dungeon, those who
>   live in darkness (Is 42:6-7).

In the New Testament, at the beginning of his ministry, Jesus presents himself in his hometown synagogue with a reading again from Isaiah - this time chapter 61 in which recovery of sight to the blind is once again mentioned as one of the signs of

Messiahship (Lk 4:16-21). When John the Baptist begins to doubt if Jesus is the one promised, he sends messengers to Jesus who responds by referring to the facts - among which was giving sight to the blind (Lk 7: 18-23).

Though literal blindness occurs often, figurative blindness is even more common. Bartimaeus has at least the advantage of realizing that he is blind, while the disciples are sometimes rebuked for not even being aware of their blindness. "Why do you suppose that it is because you have no bread? Do you still not see or comprehend? Are your minds completely blinded? Have you eyes but no sight?" (Mk 8:17-18). The Pharisees with all their knowledge of Scripture are also blind in their rejection of Jesus. In John 9 there is the beautiful account of the healing of another blind person which reaches its revolutionary climax in verse 39, "Then Jesus said, 'I came into this world to divide it, to make the sightless see and the seeing blind'." In the same spirit The Book of Revelation has a message for the Church of Laodicea (and for all of us):

> I know your deeds; I know you are neither hot nor cold. How I wish you were one or the other - hot or cold! But because you are lukewarm, neither hot nor cold, I will spew you out of my mouth! You keep saying 'I am so rich and secure that I want for nothing.' Little do you realize how wretched you are, how pitiable and poor, how blind and naked! Take my advice. Buy from me gold refined by fire if you would be truly rich. Buy white garments in which to be clothed, if the shame of your nakedness is to be covered. Buy ointment to smear on your eyes, if you would see once more (3:15-18).

Bartimaeus' ears hear what his eyes cannot see, and with a loud cry which bespeaks his whole being he shouts, "Jesus, Son of David, have pity on me!" Who knows how long he has been blind? People in Jericho took the fact for granted. In Bartimaeus' cry for help there is a ring of hope and faith; this is the chance of a lifetime - now or never! His cry is an expression of faith in Jesus; yes, Jesus could do it! Probably this incident is at the origin of the Jesus Prayer which has always been popular in the Eastern Church and has recently caught on also in the West: "Lord Jesus Christ, Son of God, have mercy on me, a sinner."

Returning to the group, we note that the pilgrims are scolding Bartimaeus and demanding that he be quiet so as not to disturb the pilgrimage. For the most part, the piety of the group appears to be such that it did not allow for this type of interruption; yet their insistence is to no avail. Bartimaeus shouts aloud the more, "Son of David, have pity on me." His faith keeps expressing itself even in this adverse situation. Jesus, in Luke 11, tells us that our prayer of petition must be persistent. He gives the example of a friend who in the middle of the night goes to his neighbor to borrow some bread. Receiving no answer to his appeal, the 'beggar' continues knocking until the neighbor responds with a supply of food. The same message comes to us in Luke 18 where Jesus tells us our prayer of intercession must be like that of the widow who wore out a corrupt judge until he gave her what she wanted. This is the insistence in prayer Jesus taught and Bartimaeus exemplifies.

Upon hearing the beggar's earnest prayer, Jesus stops. He differs from the rest of the crowd by becoming present to this man and his needs. The gospel shows Jesus always ready to give people a new start, ever believing in new possibilities, never breaking the bruised reed. No situation is ever hopeless in the eyes of Jesus. Roger Garaudy, the famous unorthodox-communist philosopher in Poitiers, is said to have made a remark about Jesus of Nazareth, in this vein "I do not know much about this man, but I do know that his whole life conveys this one message: 'anyone can at any moment start a new future'."

The crowd now seems to sense the empathy of the Lord. They too begin to take sides with the blind man, telling him he has nothing to fear. "Get up; he is calling you." Shortly before these very ones had snapped and snarled at the poor man, but once Jesus asks the man to come to him, these bystanders take on a role of mediation. Salvation comes through people. This has a two-fold implication: it means, first of all, that we need people if we are to come to Jesus; we never come to him all by ourselves. We need each other, the community, the Church. Secondly, it means also that each of us has a responsibility to bring others to Jesus. Woe to me if I keep them from knowing Jesus because of my words, my behavior or because of the inconsistency between the two. We, the Church, need to be a light to the people, a *Lumen Gentium*. This is the basic mission of any apostolate.

In their mediatory role, the group now ushers Bartimaeus to Jesus and encourages him to be unafraid. Note how the frequent assurances of Jesus: "Do not be afraid. Take courage. I have overcome the world" need to be passed on by human beings. The gospel narrative now becomes lively and clear: "He threw aside his cloak, jumped up and came to Jesus." To throw off his cloak is equivalent to giving up everything. His cloak is like a poor man's house - it is all he has. The significance of the cloak is an ancient one: "If you take your neighbor's cloak as a pledge, you shall return it to him before sunset; for this cloak of his is the only covering he has for his body. What else has he to sleep in?" (Ex 22:25-26). Bartimaeus throws it off. In his blindness he sees only Jesus - in his poverty he wants only the Lord.

Jesus now startles us with a question which seems completely superfluous. "What do you want me to do for you?" It reminds us of a similar question asked the sick man who tried for thirty-eight years to get into the pool of Bethesda: "Do you want to be healed?" (Jn 5:6). Though the questions may seem very much redundant; in reality they contain a great deal of wisdom. Not every sick person wants to be cured. Doctors know only too well that not every patient cooperates with them; consequently a cure is difficult. On the psychological level the experience is even more common. Every counselor is aware that people offer a resistance to healing which is sometimes as strong or even stronger than the desire to be healed. They may get so much out of their problem that they prefer (subconsciously) to hang on to it. It is true most of all however on the spiritual level. A certain velleity easily thwarts any real progress. I would like to do something, be a person of prayer, live poverty, be truly apostolic, but I do not want to pay the price. It is a sterile non-committal desire which fails to affect my life, but at the same time it keeps fooling me with the harmful illusion that I am a truly spiritual person. Jesus asks the question therefore to measure the sincerity of Bartimaeus' wish. What does he want

Jesus to do for him? What is the real longing of his heart? The response is whole-hearted: "Rabboni, I want to see." There is no room for ambiguity in this man's answer.

The same question is addressed to each of us. "What do you want me to do for you?" It is a very sincere question. Do I really take it seriously? The Lord Jesus asking *me* what I want *him* to do for me! It demands in response, an equally sincere answer, one that brings out the deepest of my longings. Just as Bartimaeus' faith embodied an unconditional yes to the person of Jesus, so must my reply imply a total commitment to him, a surrender without restrictions. This is the kind of faith that healed Bartimaeus; it can make us whole and holy too.

Bartimaeus' request is answered immediately; once again the Messianic sign is fulfilled, "Immediately he received his sight and started to follow Jesus up the road." This last verse climaxes the narrative. Probably it is the first time in Bartimaeus' life that he is really free to move! Yet at the very instant of his recovery, Bartimaeus uses his newly acquired freedom to follow Jesus. What better use can one make of his freedom than to bind oneself to the Lord? He followed Jesus on the road to Jerusalem where the passion would soon take place. We pray that we too always have the courage to choose Jesus, to commit ourselves to him and to follow him no matter where he leads.

APPENDIX

A brief comparison of Bartimaeus with the rich young man, also in Mark 10, follows in schematic form:

At the time of contact with Jesus:

The Rich Young Man	Bartimaeus
Rich and privileged.	Poor and deprived.
Spiritually well advanced - has kept all the commandments since his youth; is now looking for the decisive step.	All he wants is to see.

Has direct contact with Jesus; meets him on the street in a personal way.	Shouts to Jesus from a distance; is unable to see Jesus. People hinder his direct contact with the Lord; converses with him only through others.

After contact with Jesus: (the first becomes last, and the last first)

Turns away and leaves sad.	Is excited, springs up.
Goes around in a lost manner.	Becomes a follower of Jesus, a disciple.
Is a complete outsider.	Is in full communication with Jesus; shares life with him even to death and resurrection.
Remains anonymous; has no identity.	A somebody with a name and a vision.

Father of Jesus Christ,
we thank you that in him
your light came into the world,
saving us from darkness
and inviting us to the Way of Life.
We thank you that he is ever with us, if only
        we have eyes to see,
that he ever speaks to us, if only
        we have ears to hear.
Give us new eyes and new ears
to see his presence and to hear his call
in our lives and in others,
and give us the courage to follow him
to whatever Jerusalem he leads us,
today and every day, for ever and ever. Amen.

NINE

THE STONE THE BUILDERS REJECTED

"Then all the disciples deserted Jesus and fled" (Mt 26:56). This brief sentence marks a turning point in Jesus' passion; from now on he is deprived of the company of his friends and is given over to an adverse and hostile people. It also marks a turning point in the lives of the disciples. It does not mean that they do not believe in him anymore. They still do believe in him, but their faith is a limited one which has now reached its ultimate, and this changes their course of action. The desertion does not mean either that they do not love him anymore; they still love him very much but there are other things, notably their own safety, which they love even more. These other things are now definitely at stake and alter the direction in which they are going. Any deliberate limit in one's dedication to the Lord is bound to trigger a betrayal of some kind.

The latter statement seems to be applicable not only to one's association with the Lord, but to every relationship; that is to say, it sounds like a truism. That may be, but then we have to take into account that a boundary in our commitment to Jesus is of a completely different nature from one in any other commitment. Who would dare to make the unique demand that Jesus made in saying: "He who is not with me is against me, and he who does not gather with me scatters" (Mt 12:30)? If we seriously try to live up to this exacting stand of the Lord, we find

87

ourselves somewhat disconcerted when we discover that the other two synoptics have almost the exact opposite to say: "Anyone who is not against us is with us" (Mk 9:40) and "Any man who is not against you is on your side" (Lk 9:50). Confusing and contradicting as this may seem, the three passages become meaningful when we realize that the intolerant version has the singular form of the pronoun, i. e., 'me' which applies to Jesus alone; whereas, the two liberal versions have the plural form, i.e., 'us' and 'you' which refer to the community of the disciples (and to the church). In the assertion "He who is not with me is against me" Jesus claims a unique position for himself. In his regard a compromise is impossible. In all human situations and relations a compromise is usually possible and often advisable, since there we are dealing with limited values. With Jesus however it is different; whoever tries to compromise with him has already put another value on the same level and thus denied his supremacy.

These generalizations become particular now in our consideration of Jesus' trial before Pontius Pilate. In this meditation we cannot remain outsiders. We must become involved. For this we have only to remember that the trial of Jesus is still going on. The division between prosecution and defense is not just between East and West or between conservatives and liberals, nor between the consumer society and the third world. The division line runs straight through our very existence, right through our own heart. A look at Jesus in 'his hour' can clarify our choices and strengthen our commitment to him. Let us enter into this episode with an open mind and a prayerful heart.

Jesus' death sentence passed by the Sanhedrin had to be ratified by the Roman procurator; so at daybreak the priests and the scribes brought Jesus before Pilate. Immediately we are jolted into the staggering ambiguity of the scene when it is said: "They did not enter the praetorium themselves, for they had to avoid ritual impurity if they were to eat the Passover supper" (Jn 18:28). It sounds almost unbelievable, this combination of blind outrage with a meticulous observance of external rites. The letter of the law is painstakingly fulfilled while at the same time a just man is put to death through a mock trial with its foregone verdict. The description which Jesus once gave of the hypocrisy of these people is indeed to the point.

> Woe to you scribes and Pharisees, you frauds! You pay tithes on mint and herbs and seeds while neglecting the weightier matters of the law, justice and mercy and good faith. It is these you should have practiced, without neglecting the others. Blind guides! You strain out the gnat and swallow the camel! Woe to you scribes and Pharisees, you frauds! You cleanse the outside of the cup and dish, and leave the inside filled with loot and lust! (Mt 23:23-25).

How we humans can fool ourselves! How difficult to break through our own phariseeism. How many people sincerely believe that they are sincere without realizing the duplicity of their thinking and behavior. From psychoanalysis Erich Fromm makes the point that a person can honestly believe in what he is saying and yet not be sincere:

> A person can believe that he acts out of a sense of justice and yet be motivated by cruelty. He can believe that he is motivated by love and yet be driven by a craving for masochistic dependence. A person can believe that duty is his guide though his main motivation is vanity.[1]

Religious observances can serve very well to cover up injustice, envy, self-assertion, and the like. We can focus on minutiae and escape the real issues. In our affluent society we can passionately fight against (real!) instances of injustice, yet forget about the far more vital injustice of the world-scale malnutrition and poverty. Gratifying services can make us neglect a more basic duty. Man is so complicated, and the gospel is so simple. It is to the single-hearted that it promises the vision of God.

Returning to the court scene, we see Pilate coming out from his chambers to speak to the people of the Sanhedrin. "'What accusation do you bring against this man?' he de-

manded. 'If he were not a criminal,' they retorted, 'we would
certainly not have handed him over to you'" (Jn 18:29-30). The
charge before the Sanhedrin was the blasphemy that Jesus
called himself the Son of God in two very evocative and provocative Old Testament quotations (Mt 26:63-66). Being of a
religious nature, the accusation could hardly be expected to impress Pilate. So the leaders concoct a different reason - they call
Jesus a criminal. The punctiliousness regarding ritual impurity
does not extend to honesty in argumentation. That Jesus must
die is a foregone conclusion, but the arguments may vary according to circumstances. Unfair as this may be, I do recognize
this chameleon-like behavior from my own experience.

Being of a religious nature, the accusation could hardly be expected to impress Pilate. So the leaders concoct a different reason - they call Jesus a criminal. The punctiliousness regarding
ritual impurity does not extend to honesty in argumentation.
That Jesus must die is a foregone conclusion, but the arguments
may vary according to circumstances. Unfair as this may be, I
do recognize this chameleon-like behavior from my own experience.

Pilate goes back into the praetorium and summons Jesus.
Pilate was the supreme authority, and Jesus stands before him
to answer his questions. Jesus' responses are so astonishing
however that very soon the roles are switched. From now on it is
Pilate who stands before Jesus. Jesus asks *him* for an answer:
he has to choose for or against Jesus; there is no in-between
choice. Pilate looks at Jesus and finds himself reflected in the
eyes of Christ, the Son of God. He is unable to cope with this
encounter. As a high-ranking Roman administrator he has had
considerable diplomatic experience, but this state of affairs is
beyond his grasp. He was trained and skilled in compromises,
but he still had to learn that with the Son of God no compromise
is possible. He verbalizes the dilemma perfectly: "Do you not
know that I have the power to release you and the power to crucify you?" (Jn 19:10). The phrase is certainly a tribute to Latin
accuracy - it could not have been said more precisely! Given
these two options, he has to make a choice. Frantically he is
seeking a third possibility, but there is none. For the first time in
his career his expertise in devising intermediate solutions is of

no avail. He now stands before the Absolute and he will find out in a tragic way that in this case any compromise is ruinous.

Pilate is willing to do something for Jesus, but not everything, and in fact he does nothing for him. He wants to go halfway, not all the way, and so he gets nowhere. He wants to save Jesus whom he feels is a just man, and he wants to save his own reputation in Rome, possibly with an eye on his next promotion; Jesus will be the victim of this double-hearted stance. Newman has said: "Good is never done except at the expense of those who do it." PIlate is not willing to pay the full price for the good he would like to do, and so he does great evil.

Twice Pilate asks Jesus whether or not he is a king. Indeed he is, but of a kingdom which is beyond this world. He is king in the absolute sense of the word. He demands a complete 'yes' and everything else is a 'no'. Old Simeon in his blessing to Mary had already said: "This child is destined to be the downfall and the rise of many in Israel, a sign that will be opposed...so that the thoughts of many hearts may be laid bare" (Lk 2:34-35). Later Jesus himself will say in the Sermon on the Mount: "Enter through the narrow gate. The gate that leads to damnation is wide, the road is clear, and many choose to travel it. But how narrow is the gate that leads to life, how rough the road, and how few there are who find it!" (Mt 7:13-14). Every attempt to broaden the narrow path on which Jesus leads us is a betrayal of his kingship.

Jesus before Pilate is a live question put to each of us - what do you choose? How do you react? In the words of St. Ignatius: "What have I done for Christ? What am I doing for him?" *The* work that God demands from each of us is to believe in the One he sent (Jn 6:29). Every now and then God is prodding us to take the decisive step towards just this work. He disturbs somewhat our self-assurance. Doubts arise as to whether we really live up to the demands of our faith and our vocation. In a fleeting moment we suspect that our apostolic efforts indeed do show much giving of self, but at the same time function as a cover-up for what we refuse to give. In a flash we see how our prayer life is anything but a living personal relationship with God and with the One he sent. These are moments when we are invited to transcend our complacent mediocrity and to respond fully. The price is high, but it is worth it; a wholehearted belief in Jesus as Lord is life-giving and fruitful - it creates a lifestyle that builds up the kingdom of God. Refusal is fatal, a compromise impossible.

Jesus gives the procurator an important clue to his kingship which is lost, alas, on the faint-hearted Pilate: "The reason I was born, the reason why I came into the world, is to testify to the truth" (Jn 18:37). Truth here, as always in Scripture, means the ultimate, the rock on which we can build our lives, the dependability of God's love for us-as-we-are. The only purpose of Jesus' existence is to convince us of the reliability of his Father's love. The kingdom of Jesus is nothing but this love. All he wants is to bring this love home to us. Once we believe that we are loved by God in a personal, intimate, unconditional and everlasting way, the life of Jesus has not been in vain for us.

Fairness makes Jesus add an important remark: "My kingdom does not belong to this world. If my kingdom were of this world, my subjects would be fighting to save me from being handed over to the Jews. As it is, my kingdom is not here" (Jn 18:36). Jesus had given that same warning to his disciples, so that they know what the choice for him entails: "If you find that the world hates you, know that it has hated me before you. If you belonged to the world, it would love you as its own; the reason it hates you is that you do not belong to the world ...Remember what I told you: no slave is greater than his master. They will harry you as they harried me" (Jn 15:18-20). After much experience of "ill treatment for the sake of the Name", Peter can write in his first letter: "Happy are you when you are insulted for the sake of Christ, for then God's Spirit in its glory has come to rest on you" (4:14). It is true, no doubt, that faithfulness to Jesus will bring us suffering. It is equally true that this suffering can create a bond of intimacy with him that does not take away the pain and yet has an unexplainable joy in it. It will make our lives eminently fruitful in his way.

Pilate tried four subsequent attempts for compromise -each of them escalating the entanglement and the cruelty. First he tries to dismiss the whole case to Herod and to let him make the decision; after all Galilee was under his jurisdiction and moreover the tetrarch happened to be in Jerusalem for the Passover feast. "Herod was extremely pleased to see Jesus. From the reports about him he had wanted for a long time to see him, and he was hoping to see him work some miracle" (Lk 23:8). Herod seems to be the kind of person that has religion for a hobby. He had always been interested in religious people and miracle workers. Formerly he had had a remarkable contact with John the Baptist whom he had kept in prison. From time to time he would go and see the prophet: "When he heard him speak he was very much disturbed; yet he felt the attraction of his words" (Mk 6:20). This love-hate relation had not stopped him from beheading the man when he had come into a somewhat embarrassing situation at a birthday celebration. But thank heaven, this regrettable little incident had not lessened his religious interest.

His court was mundane, frivolous, flighty. His sexual life was an outright scandal; his administration utterly selfish and cruel. Yet he managed to combine all this with his dabbling in religion. Herod proves that it is possible to silence one's conscience. If I just practice long enough, I can anesthetize my conscience. A moral seediness will be the result, but it is not difficult for me to regard this as *savoir-vivre*. After a while I no longer see the stuntedness of this kind of life.

The insight that miracles are not just sensational happenings but presuppose faith was too sophisticated for the amateurism of Herod. For Jesus, Herod and his court are a dead world which he ignores completely. He does not speak one word there, nor do a thing. The longing for God and for truth is stifled to death; Jesus is simply out of place. Unable to measure up to the challenge of Jesus' silence, Herod and his friends eventually treat him like a fool; with contempt, insult and a magnificent robe they send him back. A meeting with Jesus does not necessarily unfold into a true encounter of persons.

Not only is Herod frustrated with this outcome but so is Pilate. Jesus stands before him again - a living question, demanding an all-out choice. Being a clever administrator, Pilate quickly finds another solution. There was a custom that the procurator would release a prisoner at Passover time. He will use the opportunity to let the people choose the pardon of Jesus. In that way Pilate would not have to pass a verdict and yet Jesus would be free. He counts on the masses who, no doubt, consider Jesus as one of their own. But Pilate guesses incorrectly. The people demand the release of Barabbas, a terrorist who had committed a murder. For Jesus the situation is becoming very painful. How many of these people had welcomed him with their hosannas and put their cloaks on the road as he entered Jerusalem a few days ago! How many of them he had helped with his words and his deeds! The cowardice of Pilate and the fickleness of the crowd make the last place for Jesus not just a figure of speech but a lacerating reality.

"Pilate's next move is to take Jesus and have him scourged" (Jn 19:1). We have heard the word so often; yet the horror of its cruelty is hard to imagine. The Jews restricted the chastisement to forty (minus one) lashes; the Romans had no set limit. The utter lack of justice is glibly covered up in Luke's version where Pilate diplomatically says to the priests and the people: "I have examined him in your presence and have no charge against him arising from your allegations...obviously this man has done nothing that calls for death. Therefore I mean to release him, once I have taught him a lesson" (Lk 23:14-16). Words can be stretched to camouflage a most unfair concession to public opinion. The supreme judge has lost control over the situation. He has ventured on a cataract and now the rapids carry him quickly to the bottom. His hesitant compromise is turning more and more into a total 'no'. After the scourging is over, "The soldiers wove a crown of thorns and fixed it on Jesus' head, throwing around his shoulders a cloak of royal purple. Repeatedly they came up to him and said, 'All hail, king of the Jews!', slapping his face as they did so" (Jn 19:2-3). This pitiless game was not part of the sentence; it was an addition that echoes the flippant consent of Pilate to hand Jesus over: do with him what you want.

The fourth and last attempt of Pilate to save Jesus without speaking up for him is feeble and degrading. He comes out again and says to the crowd: "'Observe what I do. I am going to bring him out to you to make you realize that I find no case against him.' When Jesus came out wearing the crown of thorns and the purple cloak, Pilate said to them, 'Look at the man!'" (Jn 19:4-5) He sounds courageous, but the people see through the facade. He hopes that by dragging the debased Jesus around the people will be satisfied and call for the halt which he dares not impose. But unlike the priests he has no grip on the crowd. They react with the chilling cry "Crucify him! Crucify him!" Of course, Pilate yields once more. "In the end, Pilate handed Jesus over to be crucified" (Jn 19:16). We shall never be able to enter fully into the feelings of Jesus when his last hope was shattered in such a blatantly unfair way. Jesus experienced every single step of Pilate's compromise as an increasingly outrageous injustice and an ever more cruel punishment. The nadir is reached within a couple of hours. "He who is not with me is against me..." (Mt 12:30). For other people it may take more time to find out the truth of this extraordinary statement, yet it will never fail to come about.

The depth of his cowardice does not prevent the Roman diplomat from putting on a show, not bad in itself, but certainly out of place here. After having failed time and again in his responsibility which he verbalized so well at the beginning ('I have the power to release you and I have the power to crucify you'), he now publicly transfers the accountability to others. It is a shallow and insincere gesture. No one can shift the choice for or against Jesus to someone else. "Pilate called for water and washed his hands in front of the crowd, declaring as he did so, 'I am innocent of the blood of this just man. The responsibility is yours'" (Mt 27:24). What a low game he plays! What a high price the Lord has to pay!

> God our Father,
> Jesus your Son is the fulfillment of all your promises.
> He was not alternately 'yes' and 'no';
> he was never anything but 'yes'.
> This faithfulness brought him to death,
> death on a cross.
> We pledge
> to commit ourselves to him completely.
> And we pray that,
> lifted up from the earth,
> he may draw us to himself

and enable us to live
our unrestricted and unequivocal 'yes'
to him in whom everything is consummated
and to you, the source of all life and love,
today and every day, for ever and ever. Amen.

TEN

THE BAPTISM OF THE CROSS

A sacrament is an outward sign which effects what it signifies. This familiar definition makes it very important to have the right view of the symbolism of a particular sacrament since this points to its actual effect. In baptism for example the true symbol is not cleansing water but immersion. Therefore the grace of baptism is not so much the forgiveness of sins as primarily a sharing in the death and new life of Jesus. The authentic prototype of our baptism is not the baptism of Jesus in the Jordan, but the paschal event of dying on Good Friday, resting in the tomb on Holy Saturday and rising to new life on Easter Sunday; from this the real meaning of our baptism is to be understood. The ancient Jerusalem Catecheses teach clearly:

> Let no one imagine that baptism consists only in the forgiveness of sins and in the grace of adoption. Our baptism is not like the baptism of John, which conferred only the forgiveness of sins. We know perfectly well that baptism, besides washing away our sins and bringing us the gift of the Holy Spirit, is a symbol of the sufferings of Christ.[1]

Paul in his letter to the Romans is even more explicit:

> Are you not aware that we who are baptized into
> Christ Jesus were baptized into his death? Through
> baptism into his death we were buried with him, so
> that, just as Christ was raised from the dead by the
> glory of the Father, we too might live a new life. If
> we have been united with him through likeness to his
> death, so shall we be through a like resurrection.
> (6:3-5)

Jesus' baptism in the Jordan is a foreshadowing of his baptism on the cross. When baptized by John, Jesus consciously accepts his mission as Servant of Yahweh with everything this entails. This is why the synoptic Gospels and more implicitly John also, quote in their account of the baptism the songs of the Servant of Yahweh as they are found in the second part of the prophet. Isaiah. These provide the script for a divine briefing of the Son by the Father. Through them the Father also identifies Jesus as the One whom the Old Testament expected. The Spirit hovers over him to anoint him for the task. Three years later on Calvary this divine mission will be fully executed and the baptism will be consummated. John the Baptist humbly insists that he is baptizing only in water and refers to a much more powerful baptism in the Holy Spirit and in fire (Lk 3:16; cf Acts 1:5). The baptism in the Jordan is a highly meaningful action, but after all, only symbolic, while the crucifixion is a consuming reality. Jesus always considered his actual baptism, not the initial one in the Jordan, but the final one on Calvary: "I have come to light a fire on the earth. How I wish the blaze were ignited! I have a baptism to receive. What anguish I feel till it is over!" (Lk 12:49-50). To the ambitious sons of Zebedee he says: "Can you drink the cup I shall drink or be baptized in the same bath of pain as I?" (Mk 10:38).

At the Jordan, Jesus mingles unobtrusively with the crowd of sinners who confess and repent. On the cross however Jesus is singled out as a criminal, publicly and officially declared a blasphemer deserving of death sentence. In the Jordan Jesus shares the sin and guilt of his people which makes him into sin (2

Cor 5:21). On Calvary sin mercilessly unleashes all its devastating horrors upon him.

The baptism in the Jordan reveals who Jesus is. The Father is there speaking with a voice from heaven; the Holy Spirit is also actively present and descends like a dove upon him. But the baptism of the cross is a far greater revelation of who Jesus is than the one in the Jordan. In John's interpretation especially, the crucifixion is the zenith of Jesus; life: "When you lift up the Son of Man, you will come to realize that I AM" (Jn 8:28). In this text Jesus appropriates the sacred name revealed to Moses at Mt. Horeb and declares that the justification of this claim will become manifest when he dies on the cross. The fourth evangelist sees the cross as the eternal throne of Jesus' glory. "Just as Moses lifted up the serpent in the desert, so must the Son of Man be lifted up, that all who believe may have eternal life in him" (Jn 3:14-15). "'Once I am lifted up from earth, I will draw all men to myself.' This statement indicated the sort of death he had to die" (Jn 12:32-33). A popularized yet profound rendition of this Johannine emphasis is the Curé d'Ars' favorite remark that the crucifix is the most learned book a person can read.

John's Gospel attaches an enormous significance to the death of Jesus - almost more than to his resurrection. The reason probably is that in John's further-developed faith-vision the unity between death and resurrection has become even more apparent than in the synoptics. So the blood and water flowing from the pierced side of the crucified Lord are given a great emphasis: "This testimony has been given by an eyewitness, and his testimony is true. He tells what he knows is true, so that you may believe. These events took place for the fulfillment of

Scripture: 'Break none of his bones'. There is still another Scripture passage which says: 'They shall look on him whom they have pierced'" (Jn 19:35-37). In John's language to 'look' means 'to see and to understand'; so once more he refers to the cross as the ultimate revelation of who Jesus is in contrast to the sketchy intimation at the Jordan.

If the crucifixion is such a manifest revelation of God's Son, we are prompted to ask: where were the Father and the Holy Spirit during the baptism of the cross? This soon develops into a very embarrassing and incisive question. Had the Father forgotten or forsaken his Son? Jesus died when he was thirty-three years old, a young age to die. He was put to death in an extremely unfair case and in an execution so utterly cruel; yet he had never done harm to anybody. He had faithfully fulfilled the mission which his Father had entrusted to him. He could honestly say that he had lived on the food of doing his Father's will and that he had always done what pleased the Father (Jn 4:34; 8:29). Yet that same Father he had served so generously now seems to ignore his Son completely. The Father does nothing to rescue his Son from his torment. He just lets him cry, "My God, my God, why have you forsaken me?" (Mt 27:46). There comes no answer. Heaven remains silent. How can God permit this? What a cruel God he is - if he exists at all!

We have to pursue our painful and bold question. Jesus was not the only one who received no answer in his agony; many people who have prayed and cried to God in their distress feel that they have not been heard either. Where was God in their plight? People in unbearable sufferings have raised their hands to God only to find out that they were reaching out into a void. Where was God? People have honestly hoped against hope that God would save them from unemployment, failure, cancer, injustice, poverty, starvation, loneliness, neurosis, incompatibility, war, but they have found no help. Where was God? "My God, my God, why have you forsaken me?" is the cry of numerous people who have felt frustrated and cheated. They have prayed, but nobody has listened. Where was God?

The question is very real and very honest. Frankly, the answer is beyond us for we venture into the mystery of God. Yet we cannot silence the question as it comes to us from the many people whose faith has become mired in it and from our own personal experience. This is by far the most common difficulty with the Christian faith in God. It is precisely the crucifixion of Jesus that puts the question in its sharpest form. He had never done anything wrong. He had been perfectly obedient to his Father and had loved everybody to the very end. Why did God not intervene in his agony?

Facing the dying Jesus we must admit, first of all, that the question could imply some hypocrisy. We humans bear the full responsibility for his death and now we ask God why he did not interfere. While we are usually very solicitous about our freedom, we now suddenly try to shift the accountability to God. Secondly, our question subtly suggests that God connived at or even wanted the passion of his Son, as indeed many Christians seem to think. Before Pilate, Jesus said emphatically that the whole intention of the Father was that the Son would convince us of his Father's dependability. "The reason I was born, the reason why I came into the world, is to testify to the truth" (Jn 18:37). The cruelty of the test is not the Father's wish but the result of our obstinacy.

The goodness of God is like a wide, full river that flows steadily into our world. The life of Jesus is nothing but the incarnation of that stream of goodness. That body of goodness clashes with the evil and sin of this world. This causes pain and suffering, scorn and injustice. All this Jesus accepted without trying to dodge it when he discovered it to be entailed in his mission. The passion of Jesus is the collision between God's goodness and the rejection of that goodness. The cross is the intersection of the two: God's love and man's refusal. Jesus is pinned motionless to that spot. The throne of grace is from now on the gibbet of the cross.

"The Father and I are one" (Jn 10:30). In a variety of expressions Jesus had repeated this intimate oneness over and over again. It is no less true during his passion. Let us not wedge the Son apart from the Father because that would destroy his whole being and all of his message. The Father remained silent just as he always endures the evil in our world. He does not rip it out nor suppress it, but through his son he places himself in the evil's very center and thus overcomes it through sheer love. On

Calvary the Father reveals himself as love which endures all evil and in that way surmounts it. The passion of Jesus is God in the absence of God, God in the antithesis of god. "For our sakes God made him who did not know sin, to be sin" (2 Cor 5:21) and so delivered us from sin. Jesus descended into hell and thus revealed that God's love is stronger than evil and death and enabled the world to receive the Holy Spirit.

The Father remained with his son in this darkest hour. In the utter external and internal desolation Jesus' affirmation still holds: "The One who sent me is with me. He has not deserted me since I always do what pleases him" (Jn 8:29). But it is a love which is beyond our comprehension. Indeed even the most hard-hearted human being would have stopped such a suffering of his son if he had had the power to do so.

> My thoughts are not your thoughts,
> nor are your ways my ways, says the Lord.
> As high as the heavens are above the earth,
> so high are my ways above your ways
> and my thoughts above your thoughts (Is 55:8-9).

It is a surpassing faithfulness of unqualified divine dimensions. At this instant it is eminently true that God is greater than we imagine. He could afford to deliver his son to death because he would still have the last glorious word: the resurrection. This is the answer of the Father's loyalty to his Son's cry. The Father safeguards his Son in his own divine way - no eye has seen nor ear heard nor has it even so much as dawned on man. His attachment to his Son is supreme. Let us not think that the Father was unmoved by the passion of his Son. The fear of falsely ascribing human qualities to God by considering him as sensitive has sometimes led to the far greater fallacy of making him insensitive. It is true that we can never adequately speak about the mystery we call God. It is no less true that to confine this mystery to a cold, rational framework can easily make this inadequacy even worse. Modern theologians speak cautiously yet clearly about a com-passion of the Father. If God's perfection is not power but love, then it belongs to God's perfection that he can suffer.

The Father was one with his Son, and the suffering is not excluded from that oneness. Calvary means a broken-hearted Father. The tradition of the early Church and of the fathers have interpreted Abraham's sacrifice of Isaac as a prototype that helps us see the incomprehensible a little more clearly. The only son, born in a unique way, on whom all the father's hope and love were founded, climbed the hill to be offered up as a holocaust. He carried the wood himself. The father accompanied him all the way in this ordeal which was even harder on the father than on the son.

The synoptics tell us that darkness came over the countryside at the time of Jesus' death. This is more than just meteorological information from the Weather Bureau. What does it mean in biblical language? It could express intense mourning for an only son as mentioned, e. g., in Amos' prophecies:

> On that day, says the Lord God,
>   I will make the sun set at midday
>   and cover the earth with darkness in broad daylight.
> I will turn your feasts into mourning
>   and all your songs into lamentations...
> I will make them mourn as for an only son,
>   and bring their day to a bitter end (8:9-10).
> Woe to those who yearn for the day of the Lord!
>   What will this day of the Lord mean for you?
>   Darkness and not light!
> As if a man were to flee from a lion,
>   and a bear should meet him...
> Will not the day of the Lord be darkness and not light,
>   gloom without any brightness? (5:18-20).

The darkness could also signify the utter bleakness of Jesus' desolation. Perhaps it is an apocalyptic way to point out the universal impact of Jesus' death. One might read it as an Old Testament motif proclaiming divine punishment. It may also express - and this is the interpretation I prefer - the unusual nearness of God. The cloud has always been the sign of God's special presence. When Jesus died the cloud covered the place as never before in sacred history, that is to say, God was never more present.

All the evil in this world - willed and unwilled - put together would form a huge mountain. Yet God is like an immense dome covering all of this terrible mass. As a rainbow, his faithfulness arcs the whole mountain. He has the last word and is able to turn all evil into good. That is why he can afford to respect our freedom, to let nature have its course and to allow the evil to happen. Precisely in the greatest of all evils, God has shown his supreme power to restore the good in a surpassing way. The cross is humankind at its worst. At the same time it is God at his best: Jesus forgiving his torturers and the Father raising his crucified Son to glorified life.

To separate the resurrection from the passion is tantamount to mutilating the gospel message. The gift of self which Jesus brought in his death, is accepted by the Father and that *is* the glorification. The faithful of all ages have sensed a connection between their sufferings and the cross of Jesus - so much so that the word cross in Christian usage came to mean human affliction. Christians in their perplexing hardships, have come to look to the crucifix. The Middle Ages had their post-crucifixes where Jesus was portrayed with all the hideous marks of pestilential disease so that people infected with this horrible epidemic could identify Jesus as one of their own. In concentration camps, in torture-prisons, and on deathrows people up to this very day have drawn crosses with charcoal on the wall or shaped them with barbed wire so as to focus on them. Numerous people have died with the crucifix in their hands uniting their agony with Jesus'. The crucifix does not explain anything; it does give perspective. It is not a theory; it remains a mystery and the outcome is a matter of sheer faith. In the depth of his suffering, man can not conjure up the name of God; God however can suggest his name through his suffering Son.

It was not just fate that caused Jesus to be nailed to the cross: "The Father loves me for this: that I lay down my life to take it up again. No one takes it from me; I lay it down freely" (Jn 10:17-18). At the beginning of the passion, John declares solemnly that Jesus was "fully aware that he had come from God and was going to God, the Father who had handed everything over to him" (13:3). Satan capitalizes on this awareness in the temptation: "Come down off that cross if you are God's son!" (Mt 27:40). Jesus was led to the cross and stayed there because he was love in a world that knows very little about love, because he was foolish enough to be love in a world that is cruel and merciless. We submit to death by force; he willed it in the ultimate intimacy of love: "There is no greater love than this: to lay down one's life for one's friends" (Jn 15:13).

In the Apostles' Creed we profess "He descended into hell". The last word is a translation of the Hebrew concept 'sheol' which means the shadowy existence that, according to Jewish thinking, awaits a person after his death. The Jews conceive it as a protracted death, an absence of all relationships and above all of God. It is a less-than-vegetative existence in utter loneliness where life can no longer be called life. Apart from the particular Hebrew conception, the truth is that death is indeed the ultimate loneliness for everyone.

In the life of each of us there is a certain amount of loneliness. We experience this as a contradiction because we feel we are meant to be together. We may play games to deny its existence, yet it is really inescapable. It creates a deep-seated anguish, that universal experience which the Germans call *angst*. *Angst* has no specific object; I cannot pinpoint what I am afraid of; yet the dread is there. Perhaps my intellect explains indisputably that there is no reason to be afraid of a particular situation, and yet my heart remains vexed. If I had to keep watch all night in a room with a dead person, my intellect would tell me that there is nothing to fear. Maybe as long as the person was alive there was some reason for apprehension, but certainly not after he or she is dead. Yet I may very well be unable to make myself do it; I might be willing, though, if someone with whom I felt secure would be with me. The latter suggests interestingly enough that what I am really afraid of is being all by myself. Loneliness is the real object of my anguish.

But now, what about a situation where nobody can possibly be with me? There would be no remedy for that dread. Such a condition is precisely what the Old Testament calls sheol: death as absolute loneliness, where no love whatsoever can penetrate. It is into this deathly loneliness that Jesus entered: he descended into hell, or as a more recent translation has it - to the dead. Now in the midst of death there is life and love. Death is no longer sheol or hell. When we die, Christ has gone before us and is awaiting us. Each article of the Creed expresses one particular facet of our faith, that is to say, one aspect of the love which God has for us. That is why Thérèse of Lisieux could use the Creed as a hymn of thanksgiving, as a *Te Deum*. 'Descended into hell' certainly fits into this pattern. It is God reaching out to us beyond the extreme. This faith changes not only death, but also life.

The baptism of the cross reveals to us who God is: Father, Son and Holy Spirit, and this revelation brings life to the full. God is total antithesis of evil and death; he is sheer love and life. When we fight the evil we have God on our side. He makes himself the guarantee that this fight will eventually be successful, that suffering need not be meaningless, that love will overcome evil, that life has conquered death. The Lord entered so fully into suffering that he is present not only in the person who suffers but also in the person who ministers to those suffering. He himself suffered for his healing others, and healed others through his suffering.

We must never abuse our faith so as to permit any suffering or injustice to continue as allegedly meritorious or gospel-like, let alone God-willed. Only after we have done all we can to effect a cure are we to speak of the meaning of suffering. At the last judgment we shall be asked the category to which we belonged: people (1) who caused suffering; (2) who ignored it; (3) who abused it for their own advantage; (4) who alleviated it. Ultimately, the Lord identifies with the least of his brothers and sisters. His baptism revealed him as one of them.

> God our Father,
> your Son accepted the mission you gave him
> and fulfilled it to the end.
> It has cost him everything he had and was,
> but it also gave him everything:
> the lasting glory of the resurrection
> and the gift of life for all of us.
> We thank you
> for the supreme revelation

of your love in his death.
We ask you in his name
to be drawn to him
and to be pulled out of our selfishness.
Give us faith in the fruitfulness of his way of life.
Teach us to live love
not as an easy word
but as a genuine, costly deed.
Thus may his mission
come to fulfillment in each of us,
today and every day, for ever and ever. Amen.

ELEVEN

HEALED BY THE RESURRECTION

"   ...Thomas was with them" (Jn 20:26). Though John uses the words in a singular context, we can apply them in a broader sense and recognize Thomas in our own company. The doubting Thomas is part of us, not only in the harmless, teasing sense of the word but also in his serious doubt of faith. An old encyclopedia describes him as "known for his despondent, gloomy character, difficult to convince". He finds it impossible to share the naive, enthusiastic faith of his fellow disciples. We are grateful to him as the one apostle who could not readily believe in the resurrection and had the courage to speak up for his incredulity. Already in the sixth century Pope Gregory wrote, "We reap more fruit from the unbelief of Thomas who was converted than from the spontaneous faith of the other disciples who did not need conversion."[1]

This meditation however is not primarily on Thomas, but rather on the risen Lord healing the apostle (Jn 20:24-29). We will contemplate how Jesus cures the man from his grief and unbelief and brings him to the joyous faith which reaches its total expression in "My Lord and my God." We hope to join Thomas in the breakthrough of his faith. We pray that his faith may teach us to see everything in the light of the resurrection. We ask to receive so much joy from the risen Lord that we shall be able to console those in distress.

109

"It happened that one of the Twelve, Thomas (the name means 'Twin'), was absent when Jesus came." Not only is he actually absent, figuratively also he is outside the community. Adamantly he rejects the paschal witness of the other disciples who have seen the Lord. That is lethal. Our faith is wholly built on the paschal testimony of the privileged witnesses. Christians are nothing but the community of those who accept this testimony. It is the risen Lord who binds his faithful together and thus forms the Church. To repudiate the resurrection witness is to sever oneself from that community. Through his denial, Thomas casts a shadow on the Easter joy of the apostles and spoils his own happiness. He is no longer 'with them', neither literally nor in any other way. He becomes a loner. We have seen it happen in every community.

"The other disciples kept telling him: 'We have seen the Lord!' His answer was, 'I will never believe it without probing the nail-prints in his hands, without putting my finger in the nail-marks and my hand into his side'." Over-statements often are used to cover up much trouble or painful doubts. In his straits Thomas dictates odd conditions for his faith. Empirically checked facts never force a person to believe nor can they constitute the foundation of belief. None of the witnesses of the gospels checked out the resurrection the way Thomas demands. These obstinate stipulations indicate just how forlorn he is.

Thomas' problem seems to be that he hangs on to the passion while already the resurrection has changed the scene completely. He lives in the dark past and denies the beaming present. A few years ago he had joined Jesus full of idealism, but in the meantime he has become bitterly disappointed and now will not or cannot relinquish his gloomy bias. Let us assume that he came to Jesus not to make a career for himself -- like those who asked for the first places in the kingdom to come -- but for a life of actual service to the people. He noted that the Rabbi from Nazareth knew the way to the hearts of people: this Jesus had a message plus the gift of speech to convey it, and above all, the works to substantiate the message. As a co-worker of Jesus, Thomas too would become meaningful to the people. With great enthusiasm and dedication he joins the disciples of the new rabbi. When Jesus after a night spent in prayer, handpicks his twelve apostles, Thomas experiences the deep satisfaction of being one of those chosen (Lk 6:15).

However, Thomas being a keen man, sharper perhaps than most of the other disciples, begins to see that the mission of Jesus is going to lead to nothing but a failure. It becomes clear to him that Jesus can no way live up to the expectations he had created. Before the rest of the apostles are even aware of the danger, Thomas sees the cross looming in the distance. Disappointment creeps into his enthusiasm and soon he becomes a frustrated man.

It is in this mood that we meet Thomas in chapter 11 of John's Gospel. The Jewish leaders in Jerusalem are already discussing their plans to get Jesus out of the way; they had even made several attempts to arrest him. Jesus and his disciples therefore have retired to a place beyond the Jordan, a safe distance from Jerusalem. He brings word from Jesus' friends Martha and Mary about their brother Lazarus, "Lord, the one you love is sick" (v 3). On hearing this the disciples become perturbed, fearing that Jesus might go to Bethany to see his friend. They are much relieved when they find that Jesus quietly remains where he is. On the third day however Jesus frightens them when he suddenly says, "'Let us go back to Judea.' 'Rabbi,' protested the disciples, 'with the Jews only recently trying to stone you, you are going back up there again?'" (v 7-8). Jesus in spite of his disciples' pleading, is determined to go; evidently no one can stop him. Then Thomas makes the concluding remark which is so typical for him, "Let us go along, to die with him" (v 16). We are finished anyway! It is only a matter of time, a couple of weeks, maybe no more than a few days. We are martyrs for a lost case. Why prolong the agony? We have no future; we are dying out. Too bad, for the illusion has been so enchanting!

Thomas remains faithful to his master, even suggesting to die with him but it is a grim loyalty. The fervor of the beginning has turned sour, yet doggedly he does not give up. When Peter is in trouble, he braces himself with heroic words: "Even though I have to die with you, I will never disown you!" "Lord, here are two swords!" (Mt 26:35; Lk 22:38). Peter's reaction to imminent defeat is frenzied; Thomas', morose. The one uses his last reserves to stage a glittering parade with banners, colors and standards; the other uses them for a self-enacted liquidation. Both are among the chosen Twelve.

In chapter 14 we meet Thomas once more. The plagued apostle brusquely interrupts the lofty farewell discourse of Jesus. On the one hand he hears the soaring words about the Father's house, heavenly dwelling places, Jesus' pledge to come back; on the other hand, he sees clearly indications of the forcible schemes of the Pharisees and the approaching disaster. The contrast is too much to bear. "Lord," said Thomas, "we do not know where you are going. How can we know the way?" (v 5). He has lost his way. All he knows is confusion and frustration; these leave no room for a cloud-nine spirituality. Let us face reality, hopeless as it is. We have to be matter-of-fact now and not indulge in exalted oratory.

Yet though these feelings of Thomas are very real, they are not the whole of Thomas. In his heart is still another sentiment -contrasting sharply with the feelings expressed. Deep down there is also a longing for the Lord, hard to describe, a spark of hope, a remnant of the original idealism. John notes repeatedly that the name Thomas means twin. The fathers of the Church did not have to wait for depth psychology to remark that there was really a dual personality in him. There was, on the one hand, the Thomas who was disappointed to the point of losing his idealism and his faith; on the other hand, there was the Thomas who longed for his initial fervor, his first love. These two personalities were in conflict and right now the pessimistic Thomas prevails. What a struggle going on in this man!

Every believer has known similar experiences. In our faith we meet with doubts; in our belief we find unbelief. "I believe! Lord, help my unbelief" (Mk 9:24). This honest prayer is by no means restricted to the father of the possessed boy. Faith is for all of us a growing reality. Gradually it overcomes incredulity and despondency until at the end of our days we make the complete act of faith. It is hopeful to observe that the opposite also seems to be true: there is belief in unbelief. There are probably glimmers of faith where incredulity is said to reign. There is certainly belief where there is doubt. Of the Servant of Yahweh it is said: "A bruised reed he shall not break, and a smoldering wick he shall not quench" (Is 42:3).

Then in chapter 20 we find Thomas missing the resurrected Lord's appearance to the disciples on Easter evening. "It happened that one of the Twelve, Thomas (the name means 'Twin'), was absent when Jesus came. The other disciples kept telling him: 'We have seen the Lord!'" (v 24-25). Thomas reacts vehemently, that is to say, the frustrated part of him now overcomes completely the other twin-self. He simply cannot tolerate the glow of the other disciples. In reaction, he becomes aggressive and almost cynical, entrenching himself in his gloom. Persons who are frustrated have a tendency to criticize in others most harshly what they wanted so dearly for themselves and have failed to attain. Envy makes them bitter. They retreat into the past, unable and /or unwilling to move ahead. In some cases a task which was taken away from us can have such an effect.

I remember a widow who had very suddenly lost her husband and was left with five children. She could not get over the loss. Often when the children were in school, she would spend hours in what could almost be called a little museum, reading old letters, brooding over pictures of long ago, treasuring souvenirs. One day the oldest son came home earlier than usual and found his mother engrossed in her collection. Before he realized the full meaning of his words he had said to her: "Mother, do you want to lose us too?" The remark was severe, but to the point. She had lost her husband; she was well on the way to losing her five children as well. The shock opened her eyes and brought her back to life. Thomas was like this widow. He could not get over the tragedy of the passion and thus he lost contact with the other apostles. It made him incapable of accepting the surprise of the resurrection and its intense joy. It made him unable to be really a part of the community. He had become a big NO.

*****

How does Jesus heal this desolate man? Of course, there would have been an obvious and ideal solution: a private appearance of Jesus to Thomas! Then he could have come back to the company unabashed. He would have had to admit, to be sure, that he had been mistaken and that they had been right, but he could have done so in an honorable setting. He could have added at once that he saw the Lord, checked the facts, talked everything over, and was satisfied with the results. Thus he would have saved face. However the Lord usually does not choose the ideal solutions. Why taunt his omnipotence which can reveal a far greater resourcefulness in his writing straight with crooked lines? He has always done famously well using second-rate solutions. That is another lesson Thomas has to learn; in fact, it is *the* lesson he needs.

"A week later, the disciples were once more in the room, and this time Thomas was with them. Despite the locked doors, Jesus came and stood before them. 'Peace be with you', he said." 'Shalom!' is the usual Jewish greeting. It means more than just an absence of war or an inner peace of mind. It implies an all-around harmony with oneself and with all others, with one's own body and with nature; it comprises joy and justice. From the mouth of the risen Lord however, it has an even richer meaning - that peace which the world can not give nor take away, the shalom which flows from the life that overcame death.

This peace the Lord is going to bring to Thomas, but only after the apostle has returned to the community. A loner cannot be helped. "We must consider how to rouse each other to love and good deeds. We should not absent ourselves from the assembly, as some do, but encourage one another..." (Heb 10:24-25). The eight days between the two appearances have been hard on Thomas and hard on the others. Coming back to the group means bowing his head. In the struggle for the upper hand the Thomas of good will scores a point on the Thomas of pettiness. For this step the Lord has been waiting. Now Thomas is ready for healing.

"Jesus said to Thomas: 'Take your finger and examine my hands. Put your hand into my side. Do not persist in your unbelief, but believe!'" Thomas must have felt embarrassed and even ashamed that the Lord reminds him so minutely of the bold demands laid down a week ago. Yet it is by no means an act of vindictiveness on the part of the Lord. Jesus is the good shepherd freeing a lost sheep from his entanglement and he does so with gentle care. The first step of pastoral concern is always to meet the person where he is. Thomas was mired in the passion; therefore it is in his wounds that the Lord contacts him. But they are now wounds in his glorified body. They identify the risen Lord as the crucified Jesus. It is one and the same Jesus who suffered defeat and gained victory. The wounds and the passion are an essential part of the glory of the resurrection just as suffering belongs to our service in God's kingdom. That connection Thomas for all his cleverness had not understood; even worse, he had resisted that link so vehemently that he had inflicted much harm on himself and on the community. The joy of Easter integrates the marks of the passion which cannot be dismissed as an evil dream. "Did not the Messiah have to undergo all this so as to enter into his glory?" (Lk 24:26).

We have all had our bad experiences and the memories of them we should take seriously. What is repressed cannot be healed. When our negative remembrances are covered up with frustration and suspicion, the light of God cannot shine upon them nor can the grace of God make them fruitful. In our bitterness we can prevent the two-edged sword of God's word from piercing through the layer of debris, from baring the secret thoughts and emotions of our hearts, and from curing what is infected. The gospel however does provide a positive context for all our human experiences if only we wish to accept it. We are given a message that can release our grief from its hiding place and incorporate it into the death and resurrection of God's Son.

The first step of the process is neither to conceal the pain nor to nourish it, but to discover that it is not an isolated reality. We have to grasp that there is more in the world than this personal suffering, this injustice, physical pain or frustration. If we do not manage to relate our grief to the suffering of so many people and communicate it to others, our world closes in on itself and places us beyond any healing. Heartache seems to have an innate tendency to turn us selfward, and it usually requires courageous efforts to overcome this self-centeredness. But once we have learned that our suffering is part of a greater whole, we can take a big step toward a cure by realizing that eventually all suffering flows into the passion of Jesus. Our crosses can be seen then as part of the cross of the Lord. It is the experience of Paul who could write to the Colossians: "Even now I find my joy in the suffering I endure for you. In my own flesh I fill up what is lacking in the sufferings of Christ for the sake of his body, the church" (1:24). To enter into this sort of vision is a powerful way to be liberated from ego-centric and sterile suffering.

By now we are ready for the next step in the healing process which is to understand that our sufferings share not only in the passion of our Lord, but also in his resurrection. Our wounds remain but they are seen now in the light of the risen Christ. They are taken up in the proper context; this gives us the strength to bear them in a fruitful and life-giving way. In an object-lesson Thomas is taught this wisdom of passion and resurrection. Disappointment is turned into joy and belief: "My Lord and my God!"

He bursts into these words of relief. It is the Easter victory of Jesus over the resentful Thomas and the final breakthrough of the believer in him. At the same time the estrangement is overcome and community restored. He has a price to pay for his celebration though; he has to give up his resentments in order to let the joy and peace flow in. That is surprisingly, a rather high price which not everybody is willing to pay. We can become so attached to our hard feelings that it is almost impossible for us to part with them. We all have probably met people who have given up almost everything, but the one thing they still cling to as their most precious possession is their bitterness. It may be rooted in something that happened twenty years ago, but they still use every opportunity to talk about it as if it happened only yesterday. It fills their minds and their hearts and leaves little room for anything else. The paschal victory of the Lord demands the surrender of these resentments, and that very well can be a great sacrifice. But the power of the resurrection that overcame death enables us to overcome also this bitterness and to offer it as a trophy to the triumphant Lord.

> "Jesus then said to him:
> 'You became a believer because you saw me.
> Blest are they who have not seen and have believed'."

This verse forms the climax of John's Gospel. His twenty chapters have prepared the way for this final proclamation. Matthew has eight beatitudes in the beginning of his Gospel; John summarizes all in this one beatitude at the very end. Peter has a parallel in his first letter: "Although you have never seen Jesus Christ, you love him, and without seeing you now believe in him..." (1:8). It is love that requires courage because we never see him, and belief which demands generosity since there is no hand to hold. Our faith is not based on what we can see: "Faith is...conviction about things we do not see" (Heb 11:1). Our faith is based on the testimony of those who have seen: "These signs have been recorded to help you believe that Jesus is the Messiah, the Son of God, so that through this faith you may have life in his name" (Jn 20:31). May this wish and blessing come true in the life of each of us, and through us in the lives of many others!

> We thank you, Father,
> for what you did for your Son:
> you made him disarm and conquer death,
> gave him life which knows no decline,
> and flooded him with all-surpassing joy.
> We thank you for what you give to us
> in raising Jesus from the dead:
> a future which has no end,
> a new meaning to all we do,
> the certainty that our hope will not be in vain.
> Give us, Father,
> the courage to live this faith without seeing,
> a full share in the joy of the resurrection,
> the simplicity to give up all that is in the way.
> We ask you also
> that this faith and joy may make us one
> as you are one with your glorified Son,
> today and every day, for ever and ever. Amen.

TWELVE

JESUS IS LORD

A Frenchman began a letter by saying, "I am going to write a long letter because I don't have time to write a short one." We are all familiar with the truth behind this paradox -- only if we have digested the whole thought content and the entire emotional experience can we say it briefly. In this respect the early Christians set a record because they could express their whole faith in two words: 'Kyrios Jesous', Jesus is Lord. Since these two words still summarize our present-day faith, let us examine their implications and explore their riches.

Jesus is Lord, period. No glosses, no restrictions! Jesus is Lord of everything. He is above principalities, powers, virtues and dominations. He is above every name in this age and in the age to come. 'Jesus is Lord' means he has overcome the world and everything in the world. He is above politics, money, scholarship, career, service, sex and whatever else one could mention. The greatest power on this earth of course is death. No matter how powerful a politician or an athlete, one day death will have won the last bout. No matter how rich the billionaire or how learned the scholar, one day death will be the greater. In saying 'Jesus is Lord' we put no limit to this dominion and include death in it. "Christ must reign until God has put all enemies under his feet, and the last enemy to be destroyed is death" (1 Cor 15:25-26). 'Jesus is Lord' implies that he con-

119

quered also that last enemy. Paul uses a Jewish parallelism in his letter to the Romans which renders this implication very clear. "For if you confess with your lips that Jesus is Lord, and believe in your heart that God raised him from the dead, you will be saved" (10:9). 'To confess with your lips' and 'to believe in your heart' are synonymous. Likewise 'that Jesus is Lord' and 'that God raised him from the dead' mean the same. Jesus is Lord because he lives a life over which death no longer has any power. Death is behind him; from now on he just lives. That marks the vital difference between the resurrection of Lazarus and the resurrection of Jesus!

Again in his letter to the Romans, Paul tells us that Jesus is Lord over any power in this world: "Who will separate us from the love of Christ? Trial, or distress, or persecution, or hunger, or nakedness, or danger, or the sword? ...For I am certain that neither death nor life, neither angels nor principalities, neither the present nor the future, nor powers, neither height nor depth nor any other creature, will be able to separate us from the love of God that comes to us in Christ Jesus, our Lord" (Rm 8:35, 38-39). Since angels and principalities, virtues and dominations may fail to duly impress us, it seems worthwhile to transpose Paul's exultation into a more up-to-date key. 'Jesus is Lord' means he is above the structures of the Church and the community, and the tensions that arise therefrom. It means that he has dominion over the past and the future, the old and the new and that he has the power to bridge them. "God has given us the wisdom to understand fully the mystery, the plan he was pleased to decree in Christ, to be carried out in the fullness of time: namely, to bring all things in the heavens and on earth into one under Christ's headship" (Eph. 1:9-10).

The glory of the Lord Jesus can give us a tremendous strength to cope with the negative in this world. Not only the history of the saints but also our own experience has shown us inspiring examples - how faith in the Lord can make suffering bearable and even fruitful. "I consider the sufferings of the present to be as nothing compared with the glory to be revealed in us" (Rm 8:18). 'Jesus is Lord' stands for a liberating faith that takes all excessive worry and fear out of our lives. Without indulging in triumphalism, it proclaims the triumph of Jesus and rightly rejoices in it.

Faith is never abstract or irrelevant but always very personal; it puts my self at stake and affects my life very much. 'Jesus is Lord' implies that he is *Lord of my life.* "None of us lives as his own master and none of us dies as his own master. While we live we are responsible to the Lord, and when we die we die as his servants. Both in life and in death we are the Lord's. That is why Christ died and came to life again, that he might be Lord of both the dead and the living" (Rm 14:7-9). Thus the paschal victory has very pertinent consequences for my personal life, and also for my death. "O my soul, be prepared to meet him who knows how to ask questions" (T. S. Eliot). 'Jesus is Lord' expresses surrender and complete abandonment to him. It says that he can dispose of me and that I want him to dominate my life so that his will and his mentality shape it. 'Jesus is Lord' stands for an eccentric spirituality -eccentric in the literal sense of the word: 'out of center', so that I am not the center of my own life; he is. It indicates (the desire) that the relationship with Jesus is the most intense and intimate of all my relations - that he is 'my life'. "Where your treasure is, there your heart is also" (Mt 6:21). All I want is to be with him for he is the great love of my life, as St. Paul says so charismatically:

> But those things I used to consider gain I have now reappraised as loss in the light of Christ. I have come to rate all as loss in the light of the surpassing knowledge of my Lord Jesus Christ. For his sake I have forfeited everything; I have accounted all else rubbish so that Christ may be my wealth and I may be in him, not having any justice of my own based on observance of the law. The justice I possess is that which comes through faith in Christ. It has its origin in God and is based on faith (Phil 3:7-9).

To acknowledge Jesus as Lord of my life means to "be rooted in him and built up in him" (Col 2:7), but this certainly does not give me an easy formula for security; it is rather a tremendous challenge to submit all priorities of my professional and personal life to the standard set by Jesus. This will probably entail more than just the correction of some minor aberrations in my course; it may demand that I turn in an entirely new direction: "You must lay aside your former way of life and old self...and acquire a fresh, spiritual way of thinking. You must put on that new man created in God's image...(Eph 4:22-24). The impact on our personal and communal lives is considerable.

Another implication of 'Jesus is Lord' is that *He can cope with everything*. "He canceled the bond that stood against us with all its claims, snatching it up and nailing it to the cross. Thus did God disarm the principalities and powers. He made a public show of them and, leading them off captive, triumphed in the person of Christ" (Col 2:14-15). The threats I face, the problems that worry me, the things that upset my life can all be integrated into the victory and the power of the risen Lord. The limitations of my health or my personality, the faults of my character will fall into place if handed over to the power of the Lord. Integration means incorporation into a greater whole. What has a malignant effect when on its own, can very well function positively when it has its proper place in the organism. "It pleased God to make absolute fullness reside in Christ and, by means of him, to reconcile everything in his person..." (Col 1:19-20). A serious doubt that weakens my faith, an unfair treatment by those in authority that tends to embitter me, a love relationship that does not agree with my marriage or my celibacy, the incompatibility of those living together, are examples of very real crises that can befall any of us. If in faith I bring such a crisis before the Lord in my prayer, it can - not without pain and sacrifice - be incorporated into my relationship with him and strengthen the bond between us. I could also withhold this concern from the lordship of Jesus and spend (perhaps much) time on it apart from the Lord. In that case the dominion of Jesus no longer embraces all of my life; the unity of it is split and eventually the split-off part will probably subdue the rest. "He who is not with me is against me, and he who does not gather with me scatters" (Mt 12:30). "No man can serve two masters" (Mt 6:24). The power that goes out from the Lord then works against me, whereas that same power can be healing and strengthening, if only I choose it to be so.

That 'Jesus is Lord' *throws light on the mystery of life.* He holds the key to its secret and lets his light shine in the darkness. The mystery of life is made lucent in him. What life is all about, the meaning and the goal of it, the way to make it worthwhile and authentic can be learned from Jesus. In fact he came to make us live life fully, as he said, "I came that they may have life and have it to the full" (Jn 10:10). John summarizes this vision towards the end of his first letter:

> The testimony is this:
> God gave us eternal life,
> and this life is in his Son.
> Whoever possesses the Son
> possesses life;
> Whoever does not possess the Son of God
> does not possess life (5:11-12).

Paul has a special, radical way to point out how the lordship of Jesus is essential for understanding life. As a Jew, and especially as a former Pharisee, he had sought the source of all wisdom in the Word of God expressed in Scripture, that is to say, in the Old Testament. He had considered God's Word richer than the experience of many elders and more precious than purest gold. Later as a Christian apostle he asserts that the Israelites still spend enormous energy and much time in studying these words of revelation. Yet he claims they understand only vaguely what these words really mean; they are like words covered with a veil. "Their (the Israelites) minds are dulled. To this very day, when the old covenant is read the veil remains unlifted; it is only in Christ that it is taken away. Even now, when Moses is read a veil covers their understanding. But whenever he turns to the Lord, the veil will be removed" (2 Cor 3:14-16). Thus Paul is emphasizing that the Old Testament culminates in Jesus as Lord and it is only from this vantage point that it really opens up and gives away all of its content.

Not only is 'Jesus is Lord' a revelation of the mystery of human existence, it also *reveals to us who God is.* The human mind and heart have ever probed the mystery of God and have presented to us 'the God of the philosophers'. Notwithstanding the awesome perspicacity and ardor that went into it, this presentation of God is too sketchy to build a life on. The Old Testament reveals much more about God as the one who committed himself in the covenant with his chosen people and worked his many marvels. He became known as the God of Abraham, Isaac and Jacob, and in the psalms we pray to this God. The New Testament however far surpasses this revelation and leads us to the Father of our Lord Jesus Christ. Eventually this title becomes the privileged name for God in Scripture. God is first of all the Father of Jesus Christ, that is to say, he is the one of whom Jesus was constantly speaking from the fullness of his heart and who shaped his life. It is this Father who made Jesus the person he is, who gave him his identity. But there is more: the full-fledged New Testament name for God is: Father of our *Lord* Jesus Christ. Thus we express our faith in the Father who made Jesus Lord, that is, who was so divinely faithful to his Son that he raised him from the dead and led him into the glory of the resurrection. That expresses the utmost of all God's marvels and by that he is named for ever; this is the God in whom we believe. Is this why Teresa of Avila complained that the lost years of her life were those in which she tried to approach God bypassing Jesus Christ.?

'Jesus is Lord' establishes the *foundation for all apostolate*. Modern life confronts us with baffling complexity. It is not easy to find the right message, the sound counsel, the discerning answer. To engage in the apostolate of the eighties requires more courage than most sensible people can muster up if it were not for the certainty that Jesus is Lord. This implies not only that he calls us to a service which is courageous, magnanimous, unconditional and unlimited, but it also means that he himself constitutes the basic security that renders this service possible at all. Obviously this does not mean that he simply gives us all the answers, but that he does show us in which direction we have to look for the right answers. We are sure of this one thing: if we bring a person closer to Jesus Christ, then we bring that person also closer to himself or herself. The reverse fortunately is also true: if a person comes closer to himself, then he also comes closer to Jesus. But the same truth can also be stated in a negative way: any service of others that diminishes their relationship with Jesus Christ is disservice to those being served. Jesus as the deepest Ground of all that exists and as the ultimate revelation of human life gives coherence to all ministry. "Whatever you do, whether in speech or in action, do it in the name of the Lord Jesus" (Col 3:17). In his discourse in Caesarea, Peter - in one of the possible translations - asserts that the content of the good news of peace is precisely that Jesus Christ is Lord of all (Acts 10:36). This is the message that must be preached and by the same token this renders it possible to preach that message.

Not only is 'Jesus is Lord' the basis of all apostolate, it is also the *foundation of all contemplation*. The rich text that forms the climax of the sharp passage at the end of 2 Cor 3 provides a beautiful illustration: "All of us, gazing on the Lord's glory with unveiled faces, are being transformed from glory to glory into his very image by the Lord who is the Spirit" (v 18). Contemplation is basically nothing but a contemplating of God's glory, a gazing on it. That glory can be seen everywhere, since all the earth is full of his glory. "To him who can see, nothing is profane" (Teilhard de Chardin). Yet of all creation we acknowledge Scripture as the privileged *locus* for the re-velation of God's glory. But then again, Paul argues, this divine glory is fully un-veiled only when a person comes to the Lord Jesus. In him we can contemplate God's un-veiled glory. Contemplation therefore is above all else, looking at the Person of Jesus. The remarkable point of Paul's statement is that this contemplation of the Lord brings about a transformation of the person contemplating.

In another letter he maintains that we are all predestined by the Father to become true images of his Son, so that Jesus will be the firstborn of many brothers (Rom 8:29). This then is realized in contemplation, where we are transformed into the image of the one we contemplate. In the spirituality of the Christian East, it is often said that one becomes that which one contemplates. Contemplation therefore achieves the ultimate goal of our lives, turning us into the persons God intends us to become. In other words, contemplation is claimed to be eminently effective. To ears inured with the idea that contemplation is not productive, this sounds strange enough. Paul's final word in this passage ascribes this effectiveness not to our own will power or efficiency, but to the Holy Spirit. The transformation takes place at such a deep level that we could never reach it ourselves; only the Spirit can penetrate and operate so intimately. The change is so profound that for quite some time it may hardly be noticeable on the surface and yet it is more efficacious than any extrinsic activity. If a person generously and honestly takes time, and time enough, to wait on the Lord, to gaze on him, to waste time with him, then even without his being aware of it, he will be transformed.

The fact that Jesus is Lord is *a source of unity* of all Christians, and beyond that, of all humankind. First, the Lord creates a unity among his followers. As Lord he puts in their places the ideas and ideals we have and counterbalances their tendency to develop into idols. If we neglect to emphasize both in belief and in action that Jesus is Lord, we dissipate our energies and our unity, just as believing that Jesus is Lord has a tremendous binding force that holds people of various opinions and lifestyles together. It is stimulating to observe how the early Church overcame all kinds of serious disagreements and tensions and survived heavy crises because beyond their divisions, they were united in the faith that Jesus is Lord. "Jesus is head of the body, the church" (Col. 1:18).

The expansion of this view, so as to include also non-Christians into the unity created by Jesus' lordship, may need some clarification. It is obvious that among those who do not consider themselves Christians there is often a deep and generous faith in God or a Supreme Being. Vatican II has stated explicitly about non-Christians: "At times there is present a recognition of a supreme being, or still more of a Father. This awareness and recognition results in a way of life that is imbued with a deep religious sense." It seems to be largely at the promptings of the mission-bishops that the Vatican Council expresses "a high regard for the manner of life and conduct, the precepts and doctrines which...often reflect a ray of that truth which enlightens all men."[1] Many of these people have hardly ever heard of Jesus and certainly they could not be said to know him. Yet we believe that their (gift of) faith is not unrelated to the death and resurrection of Jesus Christ. "The truth is this: God is one. One also is the mediator between God and men, the man Christ Jesus, who gave himself as a ransom for all" (1 Tm 2:5-6). This Christian doctrine may sound provocative. Yet it also contains an element that stimulates ecumenism and demands of us Christians to learn from other religions. This aspect was recently pointed out by someone who has much contact with and great respect for non-Christian religions (notably Buddhism); I mean William Johnston, who is Director of the Institute of Oriental Religions at Sophia University in Tokyo.

> I may sound unecumenical in that I give to Jesus Christ a unique role which I cannot accord to the founders of other religions even when I esteem them profoundly. But, after all, this is my belief, and ecumensim can only grow and develop when the members of the great religions are honest and faithful to their deepest convictions. Perhaps the matter could be stated more positively by saying that the Risen Jesus who sits at the right hand of the Father belongs to all men and to all religions. No one religion, even Christianity, can claim to understand 'the unsearchable riches of Christ' (Ephesians 3:8). That is why we need one another so that by dialogue and mutual help our partial knowledge may become more complete.[2]

Though at first sight 'Jesus is Lord' may look like a word easy to pronounce, after closer scrutiny it is clear that we need much strength to say it and to live it in fidelity. It is not just a matter of being intellectually and emotionally ready for its brevity like the Frenchman for his succinct letter. It is above all its spiritual implications that make it a difficult word since it requires a complete gift of self in a full-fledged faith. Small wonder that "no one can say 'Jesus is Lord', except in the Holy spirit" (1 Cor 12:3).

> Father of our Lord Jesus Christ,
> no one has ever seen you.

But you sent your Son to live among us.
We recognize him as one of us.
We understand his words and share his feelings.
At the same time we acknowledge
that he is more than any of us:
God from God and light from light.
In him we see you.
We admire your faithfulness and your power,
in placing him high above all the powers of this world.
Grant that we may know him
as the Lord and master of our lives,
as the meaning of our existence,
as the revelation of who you are,
as the liberator from our pettiness,
and as the source of our unity with each other,
today and every day, for ever and ever. Amen.

THIRTEEN

THE ADORATION OF THE LAMB

As Christians we rejoice in the faith that Jesus is Lord. We commemorate his life on earth, the death he endured for our salvation, his glorious resurrection and ascension into heaven, and rightly call that a celebration, a Eucharist. With grateful hearts we meditate on his words and deeds, on his personality and his Spirit, on who he was. Sometimes, as in the last two chapters, we focus on who he *is:* the risen Jesus who is Lord in the full sense of the word. In every authentic liturgy is also included an anticipation of his final coming-again and a participation in the heavenly liturgy. The meditation of this chapter will center on the adoration of the Lamb as described in the fifth chapter of the Book of Revelation. We are given there a vision of the happening at the end of time that leads into the ultimate fulfillment of history.

This Christ-to-come gives thrust and dynamics to the present age. He is the propelling force in the evolution of life and in the true development of the world. "It pleased God to make absolute fullness reside in him and, by means of him, to reconcile everything in his person, both on earth and in the heavens..." (Col. 1:19-20). Teilhard de Chardin refers to him as Point Omega, towards which all evolution strives and into which all creation eventually will be perfectly integrated. The final unity of all creation is so intimate and complete that in Teilhard's view, Point Omega is to be considered as one transcendent and autonomous Personality in whom all human persons reach maximum consciousness and full-fledged identity. The Christ-to-come works mightily here and now towards this irreversible completion of creation. He rouses a spirit of hope and expectation without which Christianity easily degenerates into an innocuous brand of optimism. If we underrate the impact of the eschatological aspect of our Christian faith, the zest is taken out of the evolution and our belief is turned from a vigorous drive into an inert coziness. The folly of the cross has come under control and the glory of the resurrection is attenuated; we ensconce ourselves in the illusion of an easy, pleasant progress towards a better world. Such a caricature of faith Marx called opium since it adapts and blinds us to the injustice and inhuman conditions in our society. It may be aroused to fight some border skirmishes while it fancies these to be major battles, but it has hardly caught a glimpse of the breakthrough for which Jesus Christ stands. It has little use for the - admittedly perplexing - eschatological discourse of for instance, Mt 24. It may speak about hope, but its petty expectation does not look beyond its own closed world. Briefly, this type of faith blends the progressive and the bourgeois.

Real evolution is a growth, a continuity which ever so often leads into a discontinuity, a leap. From time to time the smoothness is jolted by a jump. Calvary is not smooth, and if we wish to come after Jesus, we have to take up our cross and follow in his footsteps up that hill. The resurrection is not a commonplace affair; it demands that we lay aside our former way of life and old self, and acquire a fresh, spiritual way of thinking: "You must put on that new man created in God's image, whose justice and holiness are born of truth" (Eph 4:22-24). "Since you have been raised up in the company with Christ, set your heart on what pertains to higher realms where Christ is seated at God's right hand...After all, you have died! Your life is hidden now with Christ in God. When Christ our life appears, then you shall appear with him in glory" (Col 3:1-4). The last sentence refers to a future event. The looking forward to this happening is vital for our faith. Indeed the greatest upheaval is yet to come. The crucifixion and the resurrection, for all their critical importance, are forerunners of a far greater discontinuity at the end of time. "The glory to be revealed in us" makes the sufferings of the present pale (Rm 8:18).

The discipleship which Jesus demands is so radical that it is unlivable unless the Christian expects the Lord to come: "I tell you, brothers, the time is short" (1 Cor 7:29). The very last verse of the whole New Testament gives us a clue to all its books. It explains why the early Christians could live as the New Testament describes and have such an appeal to their contemporaries: "The One who gives this testimony says, 'Yes, I am coming soon!' Amen! Come, Lord Jesus!" (Rv 22:20). It expresses the hope for the parousia that makes it possible to live the gospel.

The seer of the Apocalypse describes his vision of the Lamb ready to complete the history of salvation. The Lamb is adored jubilantly by every creature while he subjects himself to the One on the throne. In his apocalyptic language the author articulates what Paul tells in more direct style to the city-people of Corinth: "When, finally, all has been subjected to the Son, he will then subject himself to the One who made all things subject to him, so that God may be all in all" (1 Cor 15:28).

> In the right hand of the One who sat on the throne I saw a scroll. It had writing on both sides and was sealed with seven seals. Then I saw a mighty angel who proclaimed in a loud voice: 'Who is worthy to open the scroll and break its seals?' But no one in heaven or on earth or under the earth could be found to open the scroll or examine its contents (Rv 5:1-3).

The scroll was written on inside and out; this suggests its extremely rich content. The closure with seven seals prevents its being read by any unauthorized person. Neither this chapter nor the next reveals to us the content of the scroll. The Lamb however will come and break the seals one by one. Each breaking of the seal is accompanied by awesome happenings which are described in the next three chapters; they prelude the fulfillment of all history.

"I wept bitterly because no one could be found worthy to open or examine the scroll." These are not tears of frustrated curiosity. In the apocalyptic imagery to open and to read mean to execute, to realize. The reason for the weeping is that no one is able to achieve the plan of God. These are tears of an intense hunger and thirst for doing what is right while at the same time being confronted with the utter powerlessness to bring it about.

"One of the elders said to me: 'Do not weep. The Lion of the tribe of Judah, the Root of David, has won the right by his victory to open the scroll with the seven seals'." Jesus is introduced into the vision with several titles taken from the Old Testament messianic expectation. This Jesus who has his roots so deep in the Old Covenant, holds the key which at the very end of time opens the book of life everlasting. Paul stresses several times that the Old Testament opens up only in Christ. "To this very day, when the old covenant is read the veil remains unlifted; it is only in Christ that it is taken away" (2 Cor 3:14; see above, p. 129). "All these were but a shadow of things to come; the reality is the body of Christ" (Col 2:17). John has Jesus say in a discourse to the Jews: "Search the Scriptures in which you think you have eternal life - they also testify on my behalf" (Jn 5:39). In this final vision Jesus is presented not only as the key to the Old Testament, but as the completion of *all* salvation.

"Then, between the throne with the four living creatures and the elders, I saw a Lamb standing, a Lamb that had been slain." The Old Testament expected a lion, but instead there comes a lamb. Indeed the New Testament stands under the sign of the lamb rather than of the lion. Among the eagles and lions which we portray in our official seals as symbols of our strength, the lamb may seem somewhat out of place. We shall have to adjust if we want to be with it. It will not be an easy switch since the Lamb is to be led to the slaughter silently, not opening his mouth, smitten for the sin of his people (Is 53:7-8). Two chapters later the Book of Revelation will present a similar inversion of images:

Never again shall they know hunger or thirst, nor

shall the sun or its heat beat down on them, for the
Lamb on the throne will shepherd them. He will
lead them to springs of life-giving water, and God
will wipe every tear from their eyes (7:16-17).

The ultimate actualization of all the prophets' promises is
accompanied not by the shepherd, but by the Lamb. No doubt
this is a very unique Lamb. He has been slain, and yet he stands
on his feet. Died and risen! The slaughter wounds in his live
body are the signs of his dignity. His passion and death have
been endowed in his risen body with an unheard-of glory. It is
this integration of his crucifixion into his glorified humanity
that gives him the key-place. The slaughter wounds express
Jesus' love which faithfully embraces both his Father and humankind till the end. The resurrection shows the Father's love
which faithfully upheld his Son even beyond death. This two-
fold love leads to what will last forever. Only by participating in
this unique love can we too bring forth fruits that will last.

"The Lamb had seven horns and seven eyes." The horn is a
sign of strength and power; he has seven of them, i. e., the fullness. The seven eyes symbolize the fullness of knowledge. This
knowledge is a creative one which achieves what it knows,
which knows by achieving. Jesus is the one who brings all creation to fulfillment by adjudicating it all.

"The Lamb came and received the scroll from the right
hand of the One who sat on the throne." The Lamb *stands*
before the One who *sits* on the throne. All beings are created by
God and stand before him. Jesus has entered into creation serving his Father. He is one of us and like us stands before the
throne. As soon as he has taken the scroll, there begins an adoration of the Lamb that spreads into ever wider circles and makes
him equal to the One on the throne.

"The four living creatures and the twenty-four elders fell
down before the Lamb." Neither the One on the throne nor the
Lamb nor anyone else tells them to prostrate. Adoration is always an act of complete, mature freedom. The twenty-four
elders are sovereign beings who wear the sign of power and
eminence: "crowns of gold on their heads." They are joyful, ra-
diantly "clothed in white garments." Honor and prestige are

theirs as they are seated on thrones placed on a floor "like a sea of glass that is crystal-clear." These supreme beings abandon all their prerogatives in adoring the Lamb. They forget about themselves, totally wrapped up in the Lamb and the unprecedented work he is going to do. The glory, the beauty and the power of the Lamb are so fascinating that with a compelling desire, they prostrate themselves, full of joy and wonder. In that act of adoration they reach the ultimate goal of their existence and their complete fulfillment.

Since adoration is the ultimate for every created being, we have to practice it here on earth. If authentic, it will stamp our lives effectively. It is the most mature of human deeds. It is best done taking the last place: the twenty-four elders prostrate themselves. Adoration goes with humility. There exists a self-intent diffidence that focuses on one's weaknesses and faults; it fails to adore God. There exists a self-conscious habit of making oneself artificially small and contemptible that forgets to regard God's glory. Both are forms rather of an inferiority-complex than of an authentic humility precisely because there is too little adoration in them. A typical side-effect of the neglect of adoration is the lack of deep joy and of a sense of wonder.

This is the new hymn they sang:

> Worthy are you to receive the scroll and break open its seals, for you were slain. With your blood you purchased for God men of every race and tongue, of every people and nation. You made of them a kingdom, and priests to serve our God, and they shall reign on the earth.

The Lamb is called 'worthy'. An external power can force me to do things I do not want to do and perhaps even to say what I do not mean to say, but it could never impose itself as being worthy. Like adoration this proclamation of worthiness is an entirely free response. The reason why the Lamb is worthy is his total sacrifice of self, his being slain. He has purchased people for God with his own blood. Once again the paschal event, with its two indissoluble components of crucifixion and resurrection, is cited as the crucial distinction. "He was made Son of God in power according to the spirit of holiness, by his resurrection from the dead: Jesus Christ our Lord" (Rm 1:4).

When the Israelites during their forty-year journey through the desert reached Mt. Sinai, they were promised by Yahweh in his first announcement of the covenant: "You shall be to me a kingdom of priests, a holy nation" (Ex 19:6). Much later toward the end of the ordeal known as the Babylonian Exile, this prophecy is addressed to the chosen people in their distress: "You yourselves shall be named priests of the Lord, ministers of our God you shall be called" (Is 61:6). This promise and this prophecy are fulfilled when the Lamb of God establishes the new and eternal covenant and makes us "a chosen race, a royal priesthood, a holy nation, a people he claims for his own" (I Pt 2:9).

This fulfillment is not restricted to the people of Israel, but includes every race and tongue, every people and nation, forging them into an admirable unity. "All of you who have been baptized into Christ have clothed yourselves with him. There does not exist among you Jew or Greek, slave or freeman, male or female. All are one in Christ Jesus" (Gal 3:27-28). The Lamb stands for a oneness that spans the whole of humankind. He wants and establishes a unity among his people which is comparable to his intimate oneness with his Father. Divisiveness blemishes the Lamb. When Paul in his first letter to the Corinthians denounces the various groups that identify themselves with Paul or Apollos or Cephas, it is not because he is for or against any of these parties, but because he is against all factionalism.

It is said that the four living creatures and the twenty-four elders sang a new hymn. When we compare it with the old hymn of Revelation 4, we find that the two songs are quite similar but differ in two significant ways. The sequence of this new hymn elaborates on these:

> As my vision continued, I heard the voices of many angels who surrounded the throne and the living creatures and the elders. They were countless in number, thousands and tens of thousands, and they

all cried out:
    'Worthy is the Lamb that was slain
    to receive power and riches, wisdom and strength,
    honor and glory and praise!'
Then I heard the voices of every creature in heaven
and on earth and under the earth and in the sea;
everything in the universe cried aloud:
    'To the One seated on the throne,
    and to the Lamb,
    be praise and honor, glory and might, forever and
    ever!'

The new hymn differs from the first in that the old one is sung only by the four living creatures and acclaimed by the twenty-four elders, whereas the new one is sung by countless voices of every creature in heaven and on earth and under the earth and in the sea. The lordship of the Lamb has no limits; it embraces the whole of creation. The Jesus who gently walked the roads of Palestine doing good and preaching his message, he is the one who is now adored without limitation in space or time. During his earthly life Jesus conscientiously restricted his mission to the lost sheep of the house of Israel, with the two notable exceptions of the healing of the centurion's servant and the daughter of the Canaanite woman (Mt 8:5-13; 15:21-28). Now his dominion includes everyone: a joy for those who love him and a comfort for all who believe in him.

The second difference is that the new song is directed in one breath to the One seated on the throne and to the Lamb. This is characteristic for the New Testament. One could define a Christian as a person who adores in one worship both the Father and the Son. The transition from the Old Testament to the New is marked by the fact that the unique and jealously-observed absolute transcendence of Yahweh is shared in the Christian faith by Jesus of Nazareth. Faithfully remaining within the monotheistic framework, we are introduced into the blissful intimacy of the triune God. In a famous letter written around 111 A. D. to the emperor Trajan, the legate Pliny the Younger cites as the reason for repressing and persecuting the Christians that they "gather before dawn on a stated day and sing a hymn to

Christ as God." One marvels at the concise and precise wording of the charge by the Roman administrator and at the same time one feels bewildered at the terrible price the early Christians had to pay for singing their hymn of adoration.

Yet they are joined by many others throughout the ages, people who are willing to give up everything to adore Christ as God. Remember the Christians behind the iron and bamboo curtains: degraded professionally, economically, socially, but steadfast in their faith with a tremendous generosity. I think of the contemplatives who have the courage and the humility to engage in a way of life that seems to offer hardly any sense of human fulfillment; perhaps without their realizing it, their lives are a most unambiguous sign of sheer faith. In Latin America and elsewhere a number of Christians abandon their privileges to join those deprived of rights in their striving for justice; regardless of the cruelties they have to endure for what is nothing but Christian they create base communities where the gospel gives hope and strength to the people. There are anonymous people in every walk of life who have heard the call of Christ and have responded wholeheartedly; it is an inspiring privilege just to meet one of them. They make visible, in their unobtrusive lives, what Jesus can effect in and through a person who is open to his action. They allow the Spirit of God to blow where it will and move along freely while the rest of us, if we are lucky, sail in their tailwind. They are signs of hope. Memories of encounters with them can be treasured as some of life's best gifts.

"Amen" is the last word of the hymn. It is a word of affirmation. With it we join with the tens of thousands in heaven and on earth adoring the Lamb and the One on the throne. With it we take our place among the Christians of the past and of the present. With it we want to share their gift of self.

> Lamb of God,
> you take away the sins of the world
> and break the seals that close the Kingdom-to-be.
> You are the crown of creation,
> radiant with your glorified wounds.
> We adore you, one in being with the Father.
> We admire you in your power

to draw people to follow you.
With them
we put our lives in your hands.
We want to serve you
with every fibre of our heart
and every minute of our time.
We rely on your power
to accomplish in us,
what our weakness could never achieve,
today and every day, for ever and ever. Amen.

FOURTEEN

YES

Adoration always implies surrender, a *fiat*. In fact adoration *is* a surrender of our whole being, a dedication of all our affection, a gift of every minute of our time. Adoration has to be lived; it commands a lifestyle. Since adoration is the ultimate, it includes everything. Adoration is a Yes, expressed with or without words during prayer, but then lived every single moment of the day and of the night. Adoration being the ultimate, also provides perspective to all that precedes; the total Yes injects meaning into everything that is encompassed by it. Three concise lines which Dag Hammarskjöld wrote in his diary in March 1956, some five years before his tragic death, offer a framework for a meditation on 'Yes'.

> You dare your Yes - and experience a meaning.
> You repeat your Yes - and all things acquire a meaning.
> When everything has a meaning, how can you live anything but a Yes![1]

You dare your Yes - and experience a meaning:
Yes is a daring word: it implies a risk and requires courage. It means a leaving behind in order to move ahead. We leave behind what is certain and we venture into the unknown. We give

up what has become dear and proceed as a free person without looking back. "None of you can be my disciple if he does not renounce all his possessions" (Lk 14:33). "Whoever puts his hand to the plow but keeps looking back is unfit for the reign of God" (Lk 9:62).

It can be very hard to really say good-bye. A famous French proverb claims it is *mourir un peu,* a little dying. It means farewell to people and to things to which we are far more attached than we realized. We give to the people with whom we live and we take from them. Somehow we are more aware of the sacrificing during the actual process, while the receiving becomes more manifest after it has stopped. It is like the various organs of the body which we easily take for granted as long as they function well; whereas we learn to appreciate them most when ill. It is only in the concrete leaving that we find out how dependent we are on the things we have collected during the years, how we have become entangled in the small world of our hands, our minds, our hearts. We have developed our own ways of enjoying and asserting ourselves in that small world, even to the point of imposing it on others. We have learned to manage in it. To leave means to cut the ego. That is one reason why we shrink from giving up the past.

Being human essentially is living in an exodus-situation. Leaving is part of life. We have to ready ourselves in many minor rehearsals for the final farewell which is the only absolute certainty of everybody's life. Apart from God everything in life is transitory: everything biological, social, political, intellectual, spiritual, etc. The refusal to accept this passing quality of life causes stunted growth, induration, and in extreme cases, neurosis. The early Christians sometimes called their faith 'the Way'. God is always greater; he keeps us continually on the move. "Here we have no lasting city; we are seeking one which is to come" (Heb 13:14). Jesus stressed that the kingdom of God requires the gift of self: "Whoever would save his life will lose it, whoever loses his life for my sake will find it" (Mt 16:25). The giving up oneself in this life is not done once and for all; it is an ever-growing gift of self and demands an increasing willingness to sacrifice.

To leave people and things behind does not mark the end; rather it opens up a new beginning in a wider context. The severing of the umbilical cord introduces the baby into the family; the leaving of the family's security challenges the adolescent to venture into a big world; the renouncing which Jesus demands leads us into the kingdom of God. The pruning is for increasing the yield. The Father is glorified in our bearing much fruit. It is not the stripped, stifled, petty life that honors him, but the life which surges to the full. Jesus leads the Way. This man-for-others appeals. The reflection of his intimacy with his Father intrigues and invites us. He calls us to follow. We do not know where his Way will lead us, but we do have an intuition that it will transform us for the better. If our hearts are cluttered with houses or land, relatives or friends, job or hobby, he is going to set us free so that we can go forward. All that remains will be: love - serving God and serving people.

The Yes is particularly scary because it is so personal. It affects the deepest in me, where I am most myself. There exists no mold for it. It is *my* Yes, such as no one before me has ever said and in which no one can really accompany me. The Yes condenses my whole self. I have to descend into the depths of my self in order to perform *the* act of my life. The person who wants always to be upheld by others could never go that far.

Yet in saying Yes, there is a solidarity with others which gives strength and inspiration. The community of all those who spoke their Yes gives us support. Outstanding is the help of Mary who is an immaculate Yes, a simple *fiat*. Above all, her Son in his absolutely unambiguous and unrestricted Yes, enables us to dare our yes: "Jesus Christ...was not alternately 'yes' and 'no'; he was never anything but 'yes.' Whatever promises God has made have been fulfilled in him; therefore it is through him that we address our Amen to God..." (2 Cor 1:19-20).

Nevertheless it remains an adventure to follow Jesus in his Yes. It entails giving up tangible security and the felt affirmation by others. It is an act of faith. Yes is a word of freedom; to be authentic it can never be forced. Ultimately it can be said only to a person, not to a thing or an institution. The German author Günther Grass once wrote an enigmatic little 'poem' to which he gave the title 'Yes'.

> This house has two exits;
> I use the third one.
> Between Anne and Anne,
> I choose for Anne.

The interpretation is said[2] to be that both exits of the house lead into meaninglessness which Günther Grass rejects. The third exit is not some*thing* but some*one*: Anne. Between Anne the saint and Anne the sinner, between Anne the beautiful and Anne the unattractive, the poet chooses the actual Anne and through her finds life meaningful. His Yes to the real Anne saves him from the existentialist void. Grass' poetic riddle rhymes well with Hammarskjöld's clear entry: You dare your Yes - and experience a meaning.

Meaning implies more than an intellectual conviction; it comprehends the whole of life. True meaning is beyond success or failure. The Way leads to the wisdom of the cross; this is a disaster which is a triumph, and a victory which is a catastrophe. The paschal mystery unites the horror of the crucifixion and the glory of the resurrection. The folly of the cross reveals the ultimate meaning. The following of Jesus leads beyond the antithesis of humiliation and elevation. The Way leads into a new realm of life where old values acquire a new perspective and where what used to be considered meaningless shows an unexpected significance. Therefore it provides a tremendous strength for making sacrifices. As long as we count the cost, seek our own comfort, fight for our position or strive for recognition we have not yet said a whole-hearted Yes nor experienced the true meaning of life.

You repeat your Yes - and all things acquire a meaning:

It is not enough to say Yes just once. It has to be repeated over and over again. We have to set out on a way and we have to carry on step by step. Our Yes is a growing reality; the further we go, the deeper and richer its content. The resistance, of course, is always there. We do not want to reiterate it in ever new circumstances. We find ourselves like Jacob resisting (the angel of) Yahweh (Gen 32:23-33). During the night he crosses the ford of the Jabbok and until daybreak he wrestles with a man whom he does not know is a divine messenger. At the end of his fight he asks for the stranger's blessing. He then receives a new name, Israel, meaning "you contended divine beings." In his struggle against God he becomes injured and keeps on limping. It is a strange, but typical story. How difficult to recognize God in his numerous disguises. How easy to consider him a threat to be fought. How often is our encounter with God, before it becomes a bow to receive his blessing, first a long, dark resistance. How much harm do we inflict on ourselves in that opposition. Every refusal to repeat our Yes does harm to our personality; it stifles our growth, eats out our joy and reduces the meaningfulness of our life. What follows are self-concern, grudges, resentment, compensations, addictions of all kinds, polarization which we stretch too far, fencing in against other people. The half-hearted Yes creates impaired persons, very much unlike the kind God wants us to be. "I know your deeds; I know you are neither hot nor cold. How I wish you were one or the other - hot or cold! But because you are lukewarm, neither hot nor cold, I will spew you out of my mouth!" (Rv 3:15-16).

The Yes has to be repeated so often that it includes everything in the past, in the present and in the future. As long as there is something in my past which I reject, there is still a screen in me that prevents my being transparent. That which I repress or resent splits my inner self, or becomes a heavy chain I drag along behind me. It may take time to really accept the suffering or the failure that came to me, maybe long ago, but it is vital that I do accept it. The Yes can create a meaning where first there was none. The repeated Yes will become more mature, more profound, more silent, and eventually it will extract light from the dark radiance from the cross. "We know that God makes all things work together for the good of those who have been called according to his decree" (Rm 8:28).

To say Yes is to accept the present. It means to acknowledge gratefully the talents and the possibilities I have without thinking all of them have to be realized. It means to accept my limitations in health, education, character, etc., while at the same time trying to overcome them. It means to transform gently the weaknessses into strength, the innate temptations into grace, the given potential into a ripe harvest. It means to say Yes to the lives of others and to give them the room and the sympathy they need. It means to accept the situation I am in and myself in that situation. To repeat my Yes will lead to self-acceptance which, in turn, will make everything else meaningful.

It is obvious of course, that the Yes is not identical with a limp settling for anything, neglecting all attempts to improve things. The opposite is true: it is only by accepting them that things can be improved. No effort born of anger, impatience or resentment will bear fruit. An example may illustrate this point. Suppose the parents of a stuttering boy have great difficulty in accepting the child's handicap. Whenever he stammers, they harshly make him repeat his words. One evening the parents discuss the situation. They both had noticed that the stuttering was becoming worse and they begin to see that the pressure they put on the boy may have something to do with it. So they decide to make no more remarks when the child stammers. Both father and mother manage to live up to their resolution, and yet they find that the speech handicap is becoming still worse. After sometime they talk things over once more and discover that in their first discussion they had changed only their policy, their external approach, but not their interior attitude. They had stopped scolding all right, but they still resented the stuttering. The boy was no longer being reprimanded, but he still felt the pressure of disappointing his parents. At this point the parents break through to a new mentality and accept the boy as he is, with his stuttering. The paradox is that from now onward, the child can slowly improve in his speech because he no longer has to. This is a real paradox: as long as the parents resentfully demanded it, progress was blocked; after the defect is accepted in peace, it begins to improve. In some cases we are simultaneously both the parents and the boy!

The Yes to the future is a stark act of faith since we do not know what we are saying Yes to. It is only the confidence in a *person* that enables us to say Yes for better or for worse. In the wedding it is the trust in the spouse, together with our faith in God that allows us to engage in a common future and to accept whatever it has in store. In ordination and in religious profession it is - over and above the reliance on the community - the belief in the living God that constitutes the basis for commit-ment. Without a strong spirit of faith, it would be utter foolish-ness to promise solemnly and forever poverty, chastity, and obedience. In fact the beauty and the testimony of the vows consists precisely in their being so explicitly an act of faith.

When everything has a meaning, how can you live anything but a Yes!

The faithful repetition of our Yes eventually leads us to the watershed where life starts flowing in another direction. The uphill climb pays off in a panoramic perspective and a gracious ease to live the Yes continuously. The pilgrim has become single-hearted and now sees God everywhere. The purity of his eye penetrates to the deepest Ground of everything and discerns all as grace-filled and meaningful. This in turn reinforces the Yes. Life has become whole and holy.

Meaninglessness implies that the various life-experiences are disconnected and therefore disconcerting. It just does not make sense! They present a void which creates feelings of des-pair. They paralyze all efforts to do something about it because they suggest that it is all useless anyway. Suicide becomes an al-luring temptation. In the realm beyond the watershed the iso-lated pieces fall into place and show a pattern never perceived before. Perhaps it is more accurate to say that the change takes place not so much in the objective reality as in our view of it. We have finally reached the vantage point where we have the right perspective. The total Yes has rendered all reality transparent and coherent. We feel like Jacob awakening from his dream at Bethel: "Truly, the Lord is in this spot, although I did not know it!" (Gen 28:16) A deep joy accompanies this experience. It is like coming home after a long, hopeless meander. That home is really the presence of God. We now recognize him everywhere, even where previously we had discerned nothing whatsoever of him. He is the bond that connects all. It is the old concept of di-vine providence which we rediscover in shining newness. Mean-ingfulness then, is not some*thing,* but some*One.*

God *has* nothing since he *is* the creator of all. He does not produce something which he then delivers. He remains the liv-ing center of all that is; without him, it could not be. In everything he gives, he gives himself as well; therefore he can be found in everything. It is only in recognizing God this way that reality acquires its full meaning, is allowed to be all that it is meant to be. The basic trust which is so vital for human well-being now extends to all of reality. "Nothing can separate us from the love of God..." (Rm 8:39). The surrender can now be complete. How can we live anything but a yes? We can join in with Charles de Foucauld in his prayer of abandonment:

Father,

I abandon myself into your hands;
do with me what you will.
Whatever you may do, I thank you:
I am ready for all, I accept all.
Let only your will be done in me,
and in all your creatures -
I wish no more than this, O Lord.

Into your hands I commend my soul;
I offer it to you with all the love
    of my heart,
for I love you Lord,
and so need to give myself,
to surrender myself into your hands,
without reserve,
and with boundless confidence,

for you are my father.

Others, to articulate their gift of self, may prefer the older prayer of St. Ignatius of Loyola at the end of his *Spiritual Exercises:*

Take, Lord, all my liberty.
Receive my memory, my understanding, my whole will,
all that I have and possess.
You have given all to me;
I return it all to you.
Do with me as you will;

> Give me only your love and your grace.
> with these I am rich enough
> and I desire nothing more.

In Luke's Gospel we find an expression of total abandonment that is still much older and took only one word: *fiat*. With it Mary chooses obedience as the pattern of her life, "Let it be done to me as you say" (Lk 1:38); through it she surrenders her body to God, and all her possessions are also included in this one act of abandonment. Said in a moment, it is spelled out in a lifetime. As a sheaf is bound in the middle and fans out towards the ends, so the life of Mary, in all its bounty, is held together by this little word. All her years before this moment flow into it and all the rest of her life flows from it. God's grace enables her to say it, and in saying it, she enables God's grace to work in her. It directs her whole being towards God and away from selfishness and self concern. It makes her completely transparent so that through her the Light in its fullness can come into the world. It creates the room God needs to become man. Jesus is the embodiment of Mary's Yes, the fruit of her *fiat;* greater fruitfulness is inconceivable. Her *fiat* in no way stymies her personality; in fact, it brings her utter fulfillment and is the prototype of all Christian fruitfulness.

> We come to you,
> Mother of our Lord and Mother of us all,
> to thank you for your Yes
> that gave us the incarnation of God's own Yes
> and brought life to its fullness.
> We ask you,
> teach us to follow you in saying our Yes
> with faith and courage.
> You know the cost of living the Yes;
> protect ours in integrity and joy.
> Ask your divine Son
> for the grace always to repeat our Yes
> with an ever-growing surrender
> and to experience how this increases
> the meaningfulness of our life.

Under your inspiration
may we help to build the kingdom of God
today and every day, for ever and ever. Amen.

APPENDIX:

TWO APPROACHES

This book is on faith as it is transmitted to us through the words of Scripture. Faith can be defined in these biblical words: "We believe in the love which God has for us" (1 Jn 4:16). The emphasis on God's love for us as we are permeates every chapter. At the end it may be useful to give a digest of some aspects of this prominence. It is meant only as a scheme which does not dispense with, but rather presupposes the content of the book. Without the latter, it could well be more misleading than helpful. A clear way, it seems, to picture the scheme is by contrasting it with an approach which is rather moralistic. However, fairness demands a word of caution. The moralistic approach and the faith approach by no means form a clear-cut opposition nor is there a water-tight division between the two. On the contrary, they merge and are both indispensable. The moralistic has its right, its value, its wisdom.

What makes this contrasting valid is the fact that there is a vital difference between a lifestyle which puts the emphasis on faith and one that focuses on morals. The danger is that a Christian becomes too much engrossed in the ethical, manufactures his own righteousness and, in fact, under-estimates the importance of faith, if not in theory at least in practice. The ideal situation would be a strong faith that incorporates and controls a sound and vigorous moral endeavor. After this precaution, the scheme will hopefully not be found too crude.

FAITH APPROACH	MORALISTIC APPROACH
The ultimate value is God's love for me as I am, and for my neighbor.	The most important issue is my love for God and for my neighbor.
Because God is good, he makes me pleasing to him and that makes me try to be good. I am loved into goodness.	In trying to be good, I am pleasing to him.
God is the deepest Ground of my being. Only what I give him is truly mine. The threat is not God, but I in so far as I do not let God be God.	God is easily seen as a threat; He demands sacrifices from me all the time. He is like a competitor: what he gains is my loss.
Sin is not to let myself be loved by God; to screen my self off from his love, mostly by over-involvement in other things or persons; an attempt to procure my own happiness instead of receiving it from God.	Sin is an attempt to fill up a gap in my life in an illicit way; a transgression of laws and regulations; a deliberate failure in my duties; a lack of love for God, and possibly a decrease of God's love for me.
Examination of conscience is primarily giving thanks to God for specific signs of his faithfulness and concern, and against that background, regret for my lack of response.	Examination of conscience is mostly a search for my shortcomings and a scrutiny of my motivation, with an act of contrition for my failures and a resolution to try harder.

Confession is focused on the pure joy which the Father experiences in my coming home after I strayed and in forgiving me; it is sharing in his joy and thus growing in intimacy with him.

Confession is centered on my sins which I have to articulate honestly and on my contrition for these sins; there is gratefulness for God's forgiveness, and relief

The cross is not willed by God but is caused precisely by my resistance to God.

The cross is imposed by God, both on Jesus and on me. I must patiently accept it from his hands.

Prayer means to let myself be loved by God, like sunbathing in his love, to contemplate God's glory in Jesus and in doing so to be transformed deeply (see 2 Cor 3:18).

Prayer is meditating on the Word of God and asking for his grace and help; it implies a fair amount of introspection with the danger of focusing too much on myself.

Abandonment is worked by God who effects it in me; I have to let myself be drawn by him.

Abandonment is psychologically (not theologically) experienced as my own effort, in which, of course, I am aware of failure.

Humility is being fascinated by God's beauty, goodness, and greatness, and a longing to be with Jesus in his hardships and in his glory.

Humility is trying to make myself smaller, it is intent on considering my own weakness and poverty.

Perfection is to live with God -- He in me and I in him.

Perfection means that nothing is lacking -- no faults, no mistakes, no defects.

Charity is the love of God which fills my heart to the

Charity is the greatest commandment, equal to the

brim, to overflowing, and from there flows out to my neighbor. It is *his* love which streams through me to others. It can be verified as *his* love by the fact that it includes the least of my brothers and sisters.

love of God, and the norm to be applied at the last judgment. It is my most important effort. Thank God it is deepening, but I still find much selfishness in myself and regret that I still cannot accept some people as they are.

Eucharist: all the many aspects meet in this core: "Do this in memory of Me". It is *He*. With his Body and his Blood he also gives me his Spirit.

Eucharist is a meal which presupposes a bond between those participating and also strengthens that bond. In sharing that meal I commit myself to genuine involvement for others.

In general: It is God's love for me that makes me holy. The emphasis is on God whom I serve.

It is my love for God that makes me holy. The emphasis is on me -- serving God.

FOOTNOTES

Biblical quotations are normally taken from *The New American Bible* (New York: P.J. Kennedy & Sons, 1970). The abbreviation JB refers to *The Jerusalem Bible* (New York: Doubleday & Company, Inc., 1966).

Chapter 1

[1]Harvey Cox, *Turning East: The Promise and Peril of the New Orientalism* (New York, Simon & Schuster, 1977), 102.

[2]C.S. Lewis, *A Grief Observed* (New York, Seabury Press, n.d.), 32, 52, 53. Original edition under the pseudonym N.W. Clerk (London, Faber & Faber, 1961).

[3]transl. by Clifton Wolters, (Baltimore, Penguin Books, 1961), 60, 65.

[4]P.G. 37: 507-508; English translation taken from A. Hamman, O.F.M., *Early Christian Prayers,* transl. by Walter Mitchell (Chicago, Regenery Co. - London, Longmans & Green, 1961), 162.

[5]Madeleine Delbrêl, *La Joie de Croire,* (Paris, Seuil, 1968), 116.

[6]Herwig Arts, S.J., *Met Heel Uw Ziel* (Antwerp, Patmos, 1978), 93-95.

Chapter 2

[1]The earliest representation of Jesus on the cross that we

153

know of is found on an ivory relic-shrine from the beginning of the fifth century which is now in the British Museum in London. Also from the first half of the fifth century is a woodcarving of the crucifixion on the front door of the Santa Sabina Church, annex to the Dominican Generalate in Rome.

Chapter 3

[1]Alexander Mitscherlich, *Society Without the Father: A Contribution to Social Psychology,* transl. by Eric Mosbacher (New York, Schocken Books, 1970).
[2]Lance Morrow, *Time,* March 5, 1979, 42.
[3]Peter G. van Breemen, S.J., *Called by Name* (Denville, N.J., Dimension Books, 1976), 53.
[4]Viktor E. Frankl, *Man's Search for Meaning: An Introduction to Logotherapy* (Boston, Beacon Press, 1966), 134.

Chapter 5

[1]P.L. 182: 247; Ep. 107:8.
[2]Paul Tillich, *The Shaking of the Foundations* (New York, Scribner, 1948), 161-162.
[3]Reninca, *Brandend Heden* (Tielt, Lannoo, 1947), 50.

Chapter 6

[1]ScG III, 122.

Chapter 7

[1]Karl Rahner, S.J., *Theological Investigations,* Vol. VII, transl. by David Bourke (New York, Herder & Herder, 1971), 15.

Chapter 9

[1]Erich Fromm, *Psychoanalysis and Religion* (New Haven, Yale University Press, 1950), 77.

Chapter 10

[1]P.G. 33: 1081. Ascribed to St. Cyril, bishop of Jerusalem from 349 to 387. For an English translation see: *The Fathers of the Church,* Vol. 64, St. Cyril of Jerusalem, Vol. 2, transl. by Leo P. McCauley, S.J. and Anthony A. Stephenson, *Mystagogical Lecture* 2, 6, (Washington, D.C., The Catholic University Press, 1970) 165-166. The passage quoted here can also be found in *Christian Prayer: The Liturgy of the Hours* (New York, Catholic Book Publishing Co., 1976), 1993.

Chapter 11

[1]P.L. 76: 1201; Hom. 24 in Ev.

Chapter 12

[1]Declaration on the Relation of the Church to Non-Christian Religions, *Nostra Aetate, 2.*
[2]William Johnston, *The Inner Eye of Love* (New York, Harper & Row, 1978), 70-71.

Chapter 14

[1]Dag Hammarskjold, *Markings,* transl. by Leif Sjoberg and W.H. Auden (London, Faber & Faber, n.d.), 110.
[2]Josef Sudbrack, S.J., in *Geist und Leben* 47, October 1974, 346-347.